Istanbul Travel Guide

2024

A Complete Pocket Guidebook to Exploring Turkey's
Jewel; Including Top Attractions, Accommodations,
Cuisines, Culture, History and Hidden Gems.

ADELINE M. CREEL

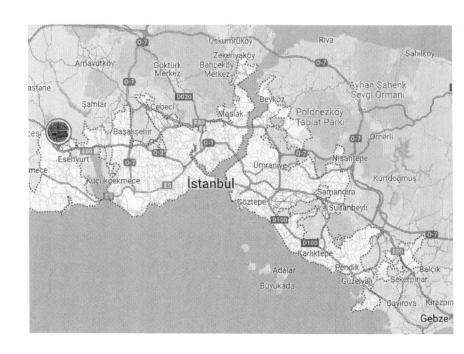

4

TABLE OF CONTENT

Introduction

Nestled at the crossroads of Europe and Asia, Istanbul is a bustling metropolis with a rich tapestry of history and culture, making it one of the world's most fascinating urban environments. This city, which was once the heart of both the Byzantine and Ottoman empires, offers a breathtaking blend of past and present, ancient and modern, resulting in a dynamic atmosphere that is both exhilarating and overpowering.

As soon as you enter Istanbul, you are swept up by the city's dynamic pulse. The air is infused with the aromas of spices, freshly made Turkish tea, and the salty breeze from the Bosphorus. The sounds of boat horns, bustling marketplaces, and lyrical calls to prayer combine to form a symphony that captures the soul of this unique city. Istanbul is more than just a tourist destination; it is a living experience.

Istanbul holds exceptional historical significance, having served as the capital of four separate empires:

Roman, Byzantine, Latin, and Ottoman. Each age has left its imprint on the city, from grand palaces and mosques to historic bazaars and public baths. As you stroll around Istanbul, you'll be following in the footsteps of sultans, emperors, and artists, with each step representing a journey through time.

The cultural diversity of Istanbul is reflected in its people and activities. It is a city where East meets West, where the Islamic call to prayer can be heard alongside the bells of a Christian church. This cultural blend is reflected in Istanbul's arts, cuisine, and daily life, making it a year-round celebration of human diversity and ingenuity.

Istanbul is the ideal destination for art lovers. The city is a living museum, with streets lined with galleries displaying excellent art by Turkish and foreign artists. Traditional arts such as carpet weaving, calligraphy, and ceramics provide insight into Turkey's rich artistic legacy.

Culinary connoisseurs will embark on an exciting adventure around Istanbul. The Turkish culinary scene is a savory monument to the city's history and location, with a wide range of meals that are both diversified and flavorful. From the rich, buttery joys of baklava to the powerful flavors of kebabs and the fresh zest of mezes, Istanbul's cuisine is a bold statement of flavor that caters to all tastes.

Despite its rich historical foundations, Istanbul is vibrantly modern. The city values innovation and progress, making it a center for business, fashion, and entertainment. The contemporary art and music scenes are thriving, fueled by the creative energies of young Turks and international artists who make Istanbul home.

What truly distinguishes Istanbul, however, is the warmth and kindness of its people. Visitors are greeted warmly and often offered tea or a shared meal. This warmth creates lasting memories and transforms first-time visitors into lifetime friends of the city.

Quick Facts About Istanbul.

Location and Geography: Istanbul is unusual since it spans two continents, Europe and Asia, separated by the Bosphorus Strait. This geographical marvel enhances not only the city's physical splendor but also its historical strategic value.

Istanbul's climate is temperate maritime, with hot and humid summers and mild to cold winters. The best seasons to visit are spring and fall when the weather is nice and the city is less busy.

Population: According to the most recent estimates, Istanbul has over 15 million residents, making it one of Europe's largest cities and the most populated in Turkey.

Language: Turkish is the official language, but English is frequently spoken in tourist areas, making communication easier.

Currency: Turkey's currency is the Turkish Lira (TRY), while many tourist facilities accept Euros.

Cultural Etiquette: Although Istanbul is a cosmopolitan city, local customs and traditions must be respected. Dress modestly when visiting religious locations, and always get permission before photographing individuals.

Safety: Istanbul is typically safe for tourists, but like with any major city, it is important to stay alert of your surroundings and take conventional measures.

Connectivity: Istanbul is well-connected both nationally and internationally. Istanbul has two international airports, many train stations, and a well-developed public transportation network, making it easy to move around.

This introduction to Istanbul allows you to see a city that seamlessly blends the ancient and modern, the traditional and contemporary. It is a location where each visit nourishes your soul, broadens your viewpoint, and leaves you wanting more. Welcome to Istanbul, a historical trip that leads to an exciting cultural adventure.

Getting to Know Istanbul

Istanbul is more than just a city; it is a phenomenon defined by its rich history, diverse terrain, and distinct cultural customs. It serves as a tribute to the richness and complexity of human culture, capturing tourists' hearts with its seamless combination of the past and present.

History of Istanbul.

Istanbul's history begins in 660 BCE when it was known as Byzantium, a little hamlet situated strategically along the Bosporus. Its significance grew when Roman Emperor Constantine the Great named it the new capital of the Roman Empire in 330 CE, calling it Constantinople. This marked the start of the city's golden age, during which it served as the center of the Byzantine Empire for more than a millennium.

During these years, the city's architectural, ecclesiastical, and cultural landscape were dramatically influenced. Iconic landmarks such as

Hagia Sophia, which was initially erected as a cathedral, represent the city's important role in Christian history. The Ottoman Turks headed by Sultan Mehmed II captured Constantinople in 1453, transforming it once more into the heart of the Ottoman Empire. The city was ornamented with magnificent mosques and palaces, including the Topkapi Palace, which served as the center of Ottoman sovereignty for decades.

Following the fall of the Ottoman Empire during World War I, the city saw another transition under Mustafa Kemal Atatürk, the creator of the Turkish Republic, who relocated the capital to Ankara. Nonetheless, Istanbul has maintained its status as Turkey's cultural and economic center.

Geography and Climate

Istanbul is strategically located on the Bosporus Strait, connecting the continents of Europe and Asia, making it a geopolitical cornerstone. The city covers an area of approximately 5,343 square kilometers, with the Bosporus separating it into two parts: the European side, which accounts for around two-thirds of the land, and the Asian side. This geographical position has been critical to its historical commerce and military strategies.

Istanbul has a temperate climate, which is heavily impacted by its peculiar geographical location. The summers are hot and humid, with high temperatures that frequently approach 30°C. Winters are chilly, damp, and snowy, with temperatures occasionally falling below zero. The city also has a reasonably moderate spring and autumn, making these seasons suitable for tourism.

Culture & Etiquette

Istanbul's culture is a vibrant mosaic, reflecting the city's numerous historical influences and role as a civilizational melting pot. The city's culture combines important parts of Byzantine, Ottoman, and modern Turkish traditions, which are intertwined into everyday life.

Hospitality: In Istanbul, hospitality is more than a practice; it is a foundation of cultural identity. Visitors are frequently greeted with kind grins and abundant tea or coffee offerings. This practice is based on a fundamental belief in the value of being kind to guests, which is influenced by both Turkish and Islamic culture.

Etiquette in Social Interactions: When meeting someone, a firm handshake is customary, but always wait to see if the person extends their hand first. Close friends and family usually greet each other with two kisses on the cheek. Use formal titles unless otherwise stated, as a display of respect.

Dress Code: While Istanbul is more liberal than other regions of Turkey, modest attire is recommended, especially while visiting mosques or religious places. It is respectful to cover one's shoulders and knees, regardless of gender. When visiting mosques, women are generally obliged to cover their heads with a scarf.

Dining Etiquette: If you are invited to a Turkish house, bringing a little gift, such as sweets or pastries, is a thoughtful gesture. It is common to remove shoes while entering a home, and meals frequently begin with everyone washing their hands. During the meal, taste a little bit of everything that is provided; this is considered courteous and shows appreciation for the host's efforts.

Istanbul's etiquette reflects its illustrious history, mixing numerous cultural traditions into a beautiful tapestry of everyday social life. Understanding these distinctions can considerably improve the experience of visiting or conducting business in this historic city.

Istanbul is more than simply its panoramic views and colorful bazaars; it is a city that has survived empires, welcomed cultures and adapted to modernity while maintaining its spirit. Istanbul, with its deep historical roots, active cultural expressions, and delicate complexities of social etiquette, provides an immersion experience into a world where the past and present coexist. As a city that has seen empires grow and fall, Istanbul invites you to walk its streets and be a part of its ongoing tale—a story as timeless as the city itself.

Planning Your Istanbul Trip

The best time to visit

Choosing the best time to visit Istanbul can greatly improve your vacation experience. The city's unique location, straddling two continents, alters its temperature, making certain periods of the year more appealing to travelers.

Spring (April-June): is widely regarded as the best time to visit Istanbul. The weather is mild, with typical temperatures ranging from 12°C to 25°C (54°F to 77°F). The city blooms with vivid colors, and the slightly off-peak tourist season allows you to explore Istanbul's highlights without the dense throngs of the summer.

Autumn (September to November): reflects the benefits of spring, with beautiful weather and fewer tourists. This season provides the ideal blend of moderate weather and the opportunity to participate in a variety of cultural activities and festivals held throughout these months.

Summer (July and August): is popular but can be uncomfortable due to high temperatures and humidity. However, it is an exciting season for festivals and nightlife. If you don't mind the heat and congestion, summer in Istanbul is vibrant and energetic.

Winter (December to March): is the least preferred season due to the chilly and occasionally rainy weather. However, for those who prefer a more relaxed stay and don't mind a little chill, winter may be a lovely time to view Istanbul powdered with snow and ready for Christmas celebrations.

What To Pack

Packing for Istanbul should be careful, taking into account both cultural conventions and the diverse activities you may engage in.

Clothing: Flexibility is crucial. Bring suitable walking shoes for exploring the cobblestone streets, as well as layers to accommodate changing temperatures throughout the day. It is respectful to bring clothing that covers shoulders and knees, such as shawls or long skirts when visiting religious buildings like mosques.

Electronics: A universal travel adaptor is required because Turkey utilizes Type C and F electrical outlets. A power bank can be useful on the go, ensuring that your devices never run out of charge during lengthy days of exploration.

health kit: Pack a basic travel health kit with medication for common diseases like headaches and upset stomachs, as well as bandages and hand sanitizers.

Miscellaneous: Remember to carry sunglasses, a hat, and sunscreen, especially if you're traveling during the summer. A tiny umbrella or a waterproof jacket can come in handy during the rainy season.

Visa & Entry Requirements

Entry into Istanbul, or Turkey in general, requires considerable forethought in terms of visas and documentation:

Visas: Many travelers must obtain an e-visa before to arrival, which is easily obtained through the Republic of Turkey's official e-visa website. The procedure is simple and can be done in a matter of minutes, as long as you have a passport valid for at least six months after your date of admission.

Passport Validity: Make sure your passport is valid for at least six months beyond the day you intend to leave Turkey. Some countries require at least one blank page for stamps.

Customs Procedures: Turkey has stringent customs procedures, particularly for the importation of medications and high-value equipment. To avoid complications at the entrance, always report things that exceed the personal use threshold.

Local Laws and Customs

Understanding and following local rules and customs is essential for a good trip to Istanbul.

Respectful Dress: Although Istanbul is relatively modern, modest attire is preferred, particularly when visiting mosques or religious places. Covering your legs and shoulders is a sign of respect.

Social Etiquette: The Turkish people are famed for their hospitality. It is usual to accept tea or coffee presented during a visit or business meeting. Refusing promptly may be deemed disrespectful.

Photography: Always obtain permission before photographing people, especially in rural regions. Certain military or government buildings may restrict photography.

Health and Safety Tips.

To guarantee a safe and healthy vacation, consider the following suggestions:

Travel Insurance: Purchase comprehensive travel insurance that covers health, theft, and loss of property. If you intend to participate in emergency evacuation or high-risk activities, ensure that your coverage covers them.

Tap Water: While Istanbul's tap water is safe to drink, it is typically recommended that you stick to bottled water, especially for short trips, to avoid stomach upset.

Emergency Contact: Familiarise yourself with the local emergency numbers. In Turkey, 112 is the number for all emergencies, which is easy to remember and useful in unforeseen situations.

Street Food: While street food in Istanbul is a must-try, look for sellers who prepare their meals fresh and have a high client turnover.

Prepare well for your trip to Istanbul to have a more fun and enriching experience. With the correct information and planning, your trip to this transcontinental metropolis will be nothing short of remarkable, full of rich historical insights, delectable culinary pleasures, and the warm welcome of Turkish people.

Transportation in Istanbul.

Istanbul's standing as a worldwide city is bolstered not only by its rich history and cultural diversity but also by its sophisticated and complicated transportation system. The city's transit infrastructure is critical for both residents and visitors, allowing for efficient and convenient movement between the European and Asian areas.

Getting to Istanbul.

Air Travel: Istanbul has two international airports, Istanbul Airport (IST) on the European side and Sabiha Gökçen International Airport (SAW) on the Asian side. Istanbul Airport is one of the world's largest and acts as a significant transportation hub, linking several global locations. Sabiha Gökçen handles both international and domestic flights and is a popular choice among low-cost carriers.

Sea Travel: Eminönü, Karaköy, and Kadıköy ferry terminals provide regular services to destinations within the city and adjacent islands. Additionally, international cruise ships routinely stop in Istanbul, bringing a large number of tourists.

Land Travel: Istanbul is well connected by road and rail. İstanbul Otogar (Bayrampaşa), the city's principal bus station, serves thousands of passengers daily, providing domestic and international connections. Transcontinental railway services, including the legendary Orient Express, connect Istanbul to European towns.

Public Transportation

Navigating Istanbul is made easier by a well-organized public transit system. The city provides a combination of traditional and modern transport modes, which are mostly handled by the Istanbul Metropolitan Municipality and other private enterprises.

Metro: Istanbul's metro network is quickly expanding, serving important areas on both continents with lines including M1, M2, M3, and

M4. The metro is a popular means of transport for avoiding surface traffic congestion.

Trams: The tram system, which includes both modern and nostalgic lines, connects popular tourist destinations and residential neighborhoods. The T1 line, for example, runs past significant historical sites such as Sultanahmet and the Grand Bazaar.

Buses: Istanbul has a well-developed bus network that operates around the clock. The city's buses connect locations that are inaccessible by metro or tram.

Marmaray and Metrobus: The Marmaray tunnel provides an undersea rail connection between the European and Asian sides, complementing the Metrobus system, which provides a fast transit lane across the Bosphorus Bridge, greatly reducing travel time during peak hours.

Ferries: Perhaps the most scenic mode of transportation, Istanbul's ferries provide a delightful way to explore the city from the water, linking several sites across the Bosphorus Strait.

Tips for Renting a Car and Driving in Istanbul.

Renting a car in Istanbul provides flexibility, but it also presents the obstacles that come with being in a crowded metropolis. Here are some suggestions for navigating Istanbul's roadways with confidence:

Rental: Use a trustworthy rental firm and look at automobiles with automatic gearboxes, as stop-and-go traffic is typical. If you are visiting Turkey from another country, be sure you have an international driving permit.

Navigation: Use a GPS or a reputable map app. Traffic congestion is a common occurrence, thus real-time traffic updates can save a lot of time.

Parking: Finding parking in Istanbul can be challenging, especially in popular districts such as

Beyoğlu and Sultanahmet. Choose hotels with parking spaces or use designated parking lots.

Driving Etiquette: Remain aware and patient. Istanbul traffic may be unpredictable, with rapid lane changes and pedestrians frequently crossing major streets.

Alternative Transport Options

For individuals seeking alternative modes of transportation or to avoid driving:

Taxis: widely available and reasonably priced. It is best to insist on using the meter to avoid being overcharged.

Bicycle: Istanbul is becoming more bicycle-friendly, with dedicated lanes and rental businesses like İsbike.

Walking: Often, the best way to discover Istanbul's varied neighborhoods and hidden jewels is on foot, particularly in old districts where streets are small and full of character.

Ride-sharing: Uber and local equivalents like BiTaksi offer another easy way to get around the city.

Visitors can improve their experience by making the best use of Istanbul's different transit alternatives, making it easier to discover the city's numerous attractions and hidden gems. Whether by air, land, or sea, getting to and around Istanbul provides insight into the city's blend of heritage and modernity, making each journey an essential part of the Istanbul experience.

Accommodations in Istanbul

Finding the ideal place to stay is critical to molding your experience in Istanbul, a city with an incredible variety of sights, sounds, and flavors. Istanbul offers a wide range of accommodation options, from magnificent five-star hotels to quaint boutique lodgings and low-cost hostels. This guide will help you choose the best location to stay, offer budget-friendly options, highlight unique accommodation experiences, and provide insights into the top tourist neighborhoods.

Choosing Where to Stay.

When choosing Istanbul accommodations, keep your itinerary, the nature of your visit, and your particular preferences for amenities and ambiance in mind. Here are some important considerations to consider.

Proximity to Major Attractions: If this is your first visit to Istanbul or you want to learn about the city's rich history, consider a hotel in or near the

Sultanahmet neighborhood, which is within walking distance of several significant historical monuments.

Access to Public Transportation: Consider how easily accessible public transport is. Staying near a Metro or tram stop might save you time and make your journey throughout the city more pleasant.

Type of Accommodation: Determine whether you want the luxury of a hotel, the comfort of a bed & breakfast, or the cost of a hostel.

View: For a more memorable visit, consider booking a room with a view of the Bosphorus or the city skyline.

Amenities: Look for features that are vital to you, such as free WiFi, breakfast included, a fitness center, or a pool.

Top Hotels for All Budgets

Luxury:

The Çırağan Palace Kempinski: located on the European shore of the Bosphorus, is a prominent hotel with exceptional service, beautiful rooms, and incomparable views of the strait.

Four Seasons Hotel Istanbul: in Sultanahmet: Ideal for those who want to wake up in the shadow of historical wonders, this hotel provides a magnificent getaway near Istanbul's major attractions.

Mid-Range:

Hotel Amira Istanbul: This hotel, located in the center of Istanbul's historic peninsula, offers outstanding service and comfortable rooms.

Pera Palace Hotel: in Beyoğlu offers nicely designed rooms with a sense of nostalgic elegance.

Budget:

Cheers Hostel: Located in Sultanahmet, this hostel has a welcoming atmosphere and is a short walk from popular attractions such as Hagia Sophia and the Blue Mosque.

Bunk Hostel: A modern alternative in trendy Taksim, ideal for those who enjoy socializing and need convenient access to nightlife and public transportation.

Unique Accommodation Experiences in Istanbul

For those looking for something different from the traditional hotel experience, Istanbul offers various unique accommodations.

Sumahan on the Water: Originally a distillery producing the famed Ottoman drink 'suma,' this boutique hotel on the Asian side of the Bosphorus provides a peaceful respite from the hectic city.

The Bank Hotel Istanbul: Housed in a rebuilt ancient bank building in Karaköy, this hotel blends elegance and historical charm, with original vault rooms transformed into elegant sleeping areas.

Neighborhood Guide with Recommendations
Sultanahmet is the hub of old Istanbul, perfect for history buffs who wish to be close to the Hagia Sophia, Topkapi Palace, and Blue Mosque. The

accommodations here range from mid-range to luxurious.

Beyoğlu: is ideal for those interested in nightlife, arts, and food. The region boasts colorful avenues like İstiklal Avenue and numerous boutique hotels and hostels.

Galata: Known for its tower and the lively streets that lead up to it, Galata combines ancient ambiance with modern cafés and stores. It's an ideal location for individuals seeking a bustling yet historical setting.

Kadıköy: For a local experience, remain on the Asian side of Kadıköy. It's less touristy and has a variety of food and retail options, as well as a youthful vibe from its huge student population.

Ortaköy: is a picturesque neighborhood along the Bosphorus famed for its stunning mosque and bustling market. Ideal for people wishing to stay in a scenic region that is away from the main tourist routes but alive and full of character.

36

Istanbul provides a varied range of lodgings to suit all types of travelers. Whether you seek luxury, a one-of-a-kind experience, or simply a comfortable place to rest after a day of seeing, Istanbul's hotel options are as diverse and fascinating as the city itself. By carefully selecting your neighborhood and style of lodging, you can improve your entire experience and have a more in-depth study of this fascinating city.

Dining & Cuisine in Istanbul.

Istanbul is more than just a cultural crossroads; it is also a culinary melting pot. This dynamic metropolis provides a variety of gastronomic experiences that reflect its rich history and the diversity of its empire-spanning heritage. From exquisite delicacies served in majestic palaces to hearty street food relished by the teeming people, Istanbul's cuisine exemplifies the city's intricate cultural fabric.

Turkish Cuisine.

Turkish cuisine is a colorful blend of flavors and ingredients from diverse regions of the former Ottoman Empire. It draws strongly on Mediterranean, Balkan, Middle Eastern, Central Asian, and Eastern European cuisines. This eclectic cuisine boasts a vast variety of flavors, from deep, smokey grilled meats to the delicate sweetness of Turkish sweets and rich, flaky desserts like baklava.

Istanbul's culinary habits have profound historical roots. The Ottoman palace kitchens in Istanbul were well-known for their extravagant food preparations, which were fed to royalty and aristocracy and eventually influenced local culinary culture. Today, these flavors can be found across Istanbul, where tradition meets modern tastes.

Must-Try Dishes

Kebaps: No trip to Istanbul is complete without trying a variety of kebaps. 'Adana kebap' and 'urfa kebap', called after their respective cities, are made of hand-minced meat seasoned with spices and grilled over an open flame.

Meze: are little morsels served cold or hot, sometimes paired with alcoholic beverages like rakı. They range from hummus and zucchini fritters to more complex seafood meals.

Baklava: This sweet dessert pastry consists of layers of filo filled with chopped nuts and sweetened with syrup or honey.

İskender Kebap: is a meal of thinly chopped grilled lamb, tomato-based sauce, and yogurt on pita bread, topped with melted butter.

Restaurant Guide (Based on Price Range and Cuisine)

Luxury Dining:

Mikla: At the forefront of Istanbul's culinary scene, Mikla serves innovative 'New Anatolian' cuisine and boasts a breathtaking view of the city from its terrace.

Nicole: Located in a historic building with a beautiful garden, Nicole serves a seasonal meal made with fresh, local ingredients and matched with an extensive wine list.

Mid-range Dining:

Hamdi Restaurant: Located only steps from the Spice Bazaar, Hamdi Restaurant offers spectacular views of the Golden Horn while specializing in traditional Turkish cuisine.

Ciya Sofrasi: located on Istanbul's Asian side, is well-known for its Anatolian meals, which provide lesser-known ethnic recipes to a wider audience.

Budget-Friendly:

Karaköy Güllüoğlu: is known for having some of the best baklava in Istanbul. It delivers a delicious, budget-friendly taste of sweet Turkish pastry.

Tarihi Sultanahmet Köftecisi Selim Usta: A traditional restaurant known for its basic but delectable köfte (meatballs) and bean salad.

Street Food and Snacks to Try.

Simit: This sesame-encrusted bread is frequently regarded as the Turkish counterpart of a bagel, and it makes an excellent snack on the run.

Balık Ekmek: literally 'fish bread', is a must-try street snack in Istanbul. It's freshly grilled fish served on a loaf of bread with onions.

Döner: one of Turkey's most famous dishes, is seasoned beef roasted on a vertical rotisserie and served wrapped in bread with veggies.

Corn and chestnuts: Roasted on the street, these are ideal for snacking while seeing the city.

Dietary Restrictions and Tips

Navigating Istanbul with dietary restrictions is manageable with enough planning.

Vegetarians & Vegans: Although Turkish cuisine is predominantly meat-based, several classic dishes, such as mezze or filled vine leaves (dolma), are plant-based.

Gluten-Free: Kebaps and most meze are naturally gluten-free, but be cautious with desserts and pastries.

Allergies: Always advise your server if you have any allergies, as nuts, dairy, and wheat are common ingredients in Turkish cuisine.

Dining in Istanbul is about experience, tradition, and the joy of sharing, not just cuisine. Each meal provides an opportunity to learn about the city's rich history and culture. Whether you want to indulge in a sumptuous lunch with a view, discover mid-range culinary pleasures, or experience the simplicity of street food, Istanbul guarantees a wonderful gastronomic trip.

The Hagia Sophia: A Monument of World Heritage

The Hagia Sophia, a majestic monument that exemplifies both architectural ingenuity and Istanbul's rich history, is more than just a place of worship; it is also a symbol of the world's great religions and empires. Throughout its 1500-year existence, it has functioned as a cathedral, mosque, and now a museum, reflecting the cultural and theological changes that have created Istanbul. This landmark structure is not just a symbol of Byzantine architecture, but also a focus of historical and architectural research.

Historical significance.

The Hagia Sophia was commissioned by Roman Emperor Justinian I and finished in 537 AD, a watershed moment in architectural history. Originally built as a Christian cathedral, it was the world's largest structure at the time and served as the Eastern Orthodox Church's principal church. The building's design revolutionized architectural aesthetics, merging a central dome with a vast rectangular basilica to create a one-of-a-kind and awe-inspiring structure.

After conquering Constantinople in 1453, the Ottoman Turks transformed the Hagia Sophia into a mosque. The addition of minarets, a mihrab, and a minbar altered its function and architectural appearance. This conversion is an important illustration of the city's multifaceted past, exhibiting a mix of Christian and Islamic elements that may be seen in its structure and décor.

The Hagia Sophia was secularised and converted into a museum in 1935, led by Mustafa Kemal Atatürk, the founder of the Republic of Turkey. This change transformed it into a symbol of secularism and togetherness, embodying Atatürk's ideal of a progressive and inclusive Turkey. However, in July 2020, a Turkish court overturned its museum designation, and it was repurposed as a mosque, provoking international debate about its cultural and historical significance.

An architectural marvel.

The Hagia Sophia's architecture is best known for its immense dome, which appears to hover miraculously atop the central nave thanks to a complex of pendentives and buttresses that disperse the dome's weight. The dome has a diameter of 31 meters and rises 55.6 meters above the earth, a marvel of engineering that impacted architectural progress in both the Islamic and Christian worlds.

The interior of the Hagia Sophia is as stunning as its structural design. The enormous nave, topped by a dome, is bordered by galleries and marble pillars, adding to its imposing appearance. The walls are embellished with mosaics, frescoes, and calligraphy, displaying creative traditions from many eras of the building's history. The golden Christian mosaics represent biblical themes and characters, while the Islamic calligraphic panels feature Quranic passages.

Cultural and Religious Significance.

The Hagia Sophia stands at the crossroads of faith, representing the historical transformations between Christianity and Islam. It is a significant emblem of religious tolerance and cultural variety throughout Turkey's history. The building's dual identity encourages discussion across cultures and religions, making it an important location for both academic research and religious reflection.

The monument's designation as a UNESCO World Heritage Site emphasizes its global importance as a cultural and historical asset. Its architecture and artistry attract scholars, architects, historians, and tourists from all over the world, making it one of Turkey's most popular landmarks.

The Hagia Sophia Today.

The Hagia Sophia is still a working mosque, and its doors are open to both worshippers and visitors, symbolizing its long-standing role as a cultural and historical bridge. The latest modifications in its status from museum to mosque have revived debates about cultural heritage preservation and the significance of such monuments in contemporary cultures.

Visitors to the Hagia Sophia are awed by its grandeur and the tangible feeling of history that surrounds the building. Whether attending a prayer session or studying its architectural and artistic elements, visitors experience a living monument that continues to inspire awe and reverence with its beauty and historical significance.

The Hagia Sophia is not just an architectural marvel, but also a dynamic record of human history. Its walls tell stories of ancient civilizations, faiths, and peoples, making it a constant source of interest and veneration. As Istanbul evolves, the Hagia Sophia remains a light in the city's historical and cultural landscape, enticing visitors to contemplate the intricate web of history it represents.

Exploring the Blue Mosque: Tips and Facts

The Sultan Ahmed Mosque, often known as the Blue Mosque, is a stunning architectural feat that reflects Istanbul's rich historical heritage. This operational mosque, erected between 1609 and 1616 during Sultan Ahmed I's reign, is not only a significant religious landmark but also a major tourist destination, attracting millions of people from all over the world to marvel at its magnificence and spiritual aura.

Historical Background of the Blue Mosque

Sultan Ahmed I commissioned the Blue Mosque to reaffirm Ottoman supremacy following the disturbing loss in the battle with Persia. Designed by Mehmet Ağa, a disciple of Sinan, the leading architect of the classical Ottoman era, the mosque aimed to rival and surpass the nearby Hagia Sophia in grandeur and beauty. The Blue Mosque, built adjacent to the Hagia Sophia, is regarded as one of the last instances of classical Ottoman architecture, combining Byzantine Christian elements from the neighboring Hagia Sophia with traditional Islamic design.

The mosque's moniker, the Blue Mosque, comes from the blue tiles that encircle the inner walls. The mosque's interior is adorned with 20,000 handmade ceramic tiles from İznik (ancient Nicaea). The tiles include a variety of tulip motifs, which are a cultural icon in Turkey and represent Allah in Islamic art.

Architectural Features

The Blue Mosque is known for its perfect proportions and majesty of architecture. The mosque is topped by a central dome and bordered by four semi-domes, all supported by huge pillars that give the edifice a flawlessly balanced appearance. The primary dome is 23.5 meters in diameter and 43 meters tall. The mosque has six minarets, which was unusual at the time because the majority of mosques had four or fewer. This architectural decision sparked criticism because it was the same number as the Grand Mosque of Mecca. Sultan Ahmed overcame this by funding a seventh minaret for the Mecca mosque.

Interior Beauty

The mosque's interior is stunningly magnificent, illuminated by 260 windows that were formerly filled with 17th-century stained glass. Unfortunately, this glass has been lost throughout time and replaced by contemporary equivalents. The upper levels of the interior are dominated by blue paint, which lends the mosque its popular name. At night, blue lights illuminate the mosque's five major domes, six minarets, and eight subsidiary domes.

The floor is covered with carpets contributed by devoted followers and replaced regularly as they wear out. The mihrab, an indented enclosure denoting the direction of Mecca, and the minbar, where the imam delivers his sermon, are intricately carved and of great religious significance.

Visiting the Blue Mosque.

Tip for Visitors:

Clothing Appropriately: As a house of religion, all guests must follow a modest clothing code. This means that legs and shoulders should be covered, and ladies must cover their heads before entering. Scarves are available at the door for individuals who do not own one.

When to Visit: The mosque is closed to non-worshipers for half an hour during the five daily prayers. It is advisable to visit in the morning or late afternoon to avoid tourist crowds and see the mosque in a more peaceful setting.

Respect the Space: Although the mosque is a popular tourist destination, it is crucial to remember that it is a place of worship. Visitors should keep a polite demeanor, speak quietly, and avoid taking photographs during prayer times.

Explore with a Guide: Consider hiring a guide who can provide detailed information about the mosque's history and architecture, increasing your understanding of this important cultural relic.

Cultural and Religious Significance.

The Blue Mosque remains an important religious center for the Muslim community in Istanbul. It is a symbol of Islamic pride and continues to be a gathering place for hundreds of people to pray, particularly during the holy month of Ramadan and other important religious festivals. For non-Muslim visitors, the mosque provides a significant insight into Istanbul's spiritual and cultural character, and thus Turkey as a whole.

The Blue Mosque not only enhances Istanbul's skyline but also contributes to the city's cultural and spiritual landscape. It continues to serve as a bridge between the past and the present, symbolizing a mighty empire's spiritual and architectural goals. Visitors leave with a sense of wonder and a better understanding of Istanbul's rich history and religious significance, making the Blue Mosque a must-see on every trip itinerary.

Topkapı Palace: The Heart of the Ottoman Empire

Topkapı Palace, a famous symbol of Istanbul's rich history, represents the grandeur and intricacy of the Ottoman Empire. The palace, built between 1460 and 1478 on the orders of Sultan Mehmed II following his conquest of Constantinople, served as the administrative center and royal seat of the Ottoman sultans for over four centuries. Topkapı Palace, with its stunning architecture, rich artifact collections, and well-maintained courtyards and gardens, provides a glimpse into the luxury and power of one of history's most fascinating dynasties.

Historical significance.

Topkapı Palace housed the empire's highest executive and judicial council, in addition to serving as the sultan's palace. The palace complex is strategically located on Seraglio Point, a promontory overlooking the Golden Horn and the Sea of Marmara, with the Bosphorus in full view. This location represented the

Ottomans' control and management over their dominions, which extended from the Balkans to the borders of the Persian Empire.

The palace grew over time, with succeeding sultans extending and adding structures, such as the Harem, which housed the sultan's wives, concubines, and children and became an important and influential portion of the palace. Topkapı exemplifies Islamic and Ottoman architecture and design, with delicate tile work, beautiful gardens, and chambers with expansive views and inner courtyards reflecting the era's aesthetic preferences.

An architectural marvel.

Topkapı Palace is a huge structure made up of four main courtyards, each with various uses, and several smaller buildings linked to them. Its architecture combines numerous styles, including Islamic, Middle Eastern, and Byzantine influences, reflecting the Ottoman Empire's eclectic spirit.

The Imperial Gate (Bâb-ı Hümâyûn): is the primary entrance to the complex, with calligraphic inscriptions and leading to the First Courtyard, which was open to the public.

The Second Courtyard: The Second Courtyard houses the administrative arm of the empire. The Gate of Salutation, ornamented with a double-headed eagle, leads to the inner sanctum, where the Imperial Council deliberated in the Council Chamber.

The Third Courtyard: This is the palace's most private and sacred area, containing the Sultan's private quarters and the treasury, which displays an outstanding collection of artifacts, including the Prophet Muhammad's cloak and sword.

The Fourth Courtyard: also known as the Imperial Gardens, features pavilions, kiosks, and terraces. It was created for the Sultan's personal and recreational use and provides breathtaking views of the Bosphorus.

The Harem

Topkapı Palace's Harem, a maze of over 400 apartments housing the sultan's wives, concubines, children, and servants, is a fascinating feature. This private area is lavishly adorned with blue and white tiles, gold and mother-of-pearl inlaid furniture, and luxuriant carpeting. The Harem was essentially a tiny universe unto itself, complete with mosques, hammams (baths), and laundry facilities. It was ruled by the Queen Mother (Valide Sultan), who was heavily involved in palace politics and succession.

Art and Artefacts.

Topkapı Palace is known for its huge collection of holy relics and gem-studded artifacts, notably the Topkapı Dagger and the Spoonmaker's Diamond, one of the world's largest diamonds. The palace also houses an extensive collection of Islamic calligraphy, religious writings, and murals, as well as Ottoman attire, weapons, and armor.

Visit Topkapı Palace.

Topkapı Palace offers both an educational experience regarding the Ottoman Empire's political, cultural, and artistic accomplishments, as well as a glimpse into its rich past. The palace is open to the public as a museum, with guided tours to provide historical context and highlight the significance of the artifacts on show. Each area of the palace provides a unique look into the sultans' lives, ranging from lavish public festivities in the courtyards to the secluded grandeur of the Harem.

The visit would be incomplete without strolling around the palace's gardens and admiring the magnificent views of Istanbul and the Bosphorus Strait. The peacefulness of the gardens contrasts with the city's bustling vitality, providing a peaceful respite as well as a chance to contemplate the Ottoman Empire's history and legacy.

Topkapı Palace is a cultural and architectural masterpiece that showcases the sophisticated court life of Ottoman sultans. Its extensive collection of artifacts, breathtaking architectural elements, and the historic narrative that runs through its chambers and halls make it a must-see for everyone interested in Istanbul's deep history, culture, and art.

The Grand Bazaar: Shopping and Exploration

Nestled in the heart of Istanbul, the Grand Bazaar is more than simply a bazaar; it's a thriving hub of business, culture, and history. The Grand Bazaar, one of the world's largest and oldest covered markets, has been the heart of Istanbul for centuries, selling everything from traditional artifacts and handmade crafts to precious metals and delicate textiles. With over 60 streets and over 4,000 businesses, the bazaar attracts between 250,000 and 400,000 visitors per day, making it a must-see attraction for tourists and a beloved spot for locals.

Historical Background.

Shortly after the Ottoman conquest of Constantinople, Sultan Mehmed the Conqueror ordered the construction of the Grand Bazaar to begin in 1455. Initially established as a small warehouse (bedesten), it quickly expanded due to its strategic location on the Silk Road trade routes, eventually becoming a busy trading hub. Over the years, it has undergone several restorations and extensions, surviving earthquakes, fires, and other natural disasters, each time rising with new layers of history and culture.

An architectural marvel.

The design of the Grand Bazaar reflects several periods of Ottoman history, with its huge network of vaulted brick roofs, sturdy walls, and hundreds of domed ceilings. The primary building is made up of two enormous covered markets (Bedesten): the Inner Bedesten (or Cevahir Bedesten), which offered the most costly commodities and antiques, and the Sandal Bedesten, which traditionally dealt mostly in textiles.

The bazaar's arrangement is not random but rather intentionally planned to maximize the flow of goods and people. The streets are organized by product type, with sections dedicated to leather products, gold and silver jewelry, carpets, spices, and pottery.

This organization not only helps customers but also maintains old crafts and practices.

Cultural Significance

The Grand Bazaar is more than just a shopping destination; it is a cultural icon that provides insight into Turkish culture and traditions. It functions as a social hub, where individuals may meet, interact, share news, and conduct commerce. The bazaar culture values negotiating ('pazarlık'), and bargaining is expected as part of the purchasing experience.

Tea stores and tiny cafés are scattered around the market, where shopkeepers and customers can enjoy a cup of Turkish tea or coffee. These locations act as social hubs, where stories are shared and friendships are formed. The bazaar also provides work for numerous artisans and traders, making it an important element of the local economy.

Shopping at the Grand Bazaar

Shopping in the Grand Bazaar is an adventure. It provides an almost limitless variety of products. Here are some must-purchase items:

Carpets and Kilims: Turkish carpets and kilims are world-renowned for their quality and craftsmanship. The bazaar provides a wide selection of possibilities, from antique hand-woven pieces to modern styles.

Jewellery: Goldsmiths' Street in the bazaar is well-known for its gold and silver jewelry embellished with precious stones. Each piece showcases the delicate craftsmanship of local craftspeople.

Spices and Delicacies: For culinary connoisseurs, spice shops provide a wealth of possibilities, including saffron, mint, thyme, and the well-known Turkish delight.

Ceramics and Copperware: Beautifully painted ceramics and hand-pounded copperware showcase Turkey's rich artisan traditions.

Textiles & Garments: The market is a textile heaven, with beautiful silks, cotton, and wool materials. Traditional clothing, scarves, and shawls are also popular buys.

Tips for Visitors:

When to Visit: The bazaar is open Monday through Saturday from 9:00 a.m. to 7:00 p.m. Visit early in the morning to escape the throng.

Bargaining: is normal and part of the enjoyment of shopping. Begin by offering half the asking price and negotiating from there.

Currency: Prices are frequently displayed in Euros or US dollars, however paying in Turkish Lira might sometimes result in a better price.

Guided Tours: For your first visit, consider taking a guided tour to assist you navigate the bazaar's wide passageways and learn about its history and offerings.

Stay Alert: While the bazaar is generally safe, it is always a good idea to keep an eye on your possessions in crowded places.

The Grand Bazaar is more than just a shopping destination; it's also an experience. It is a site where history, culture, and business blend perfectly, providing a sensory trip through distinctive Turkish smells, sights, and sounds. Each visit to the bazaar yields new insights into Istanbul's customs and daily life. Whether you're a seasoned shopper looking for magnificent antiques and crafts, or a first-time visitor eager to take up the vibrant atmosphere, the Grand Bazaar provides a one-of-a-kind and unforgettable experience.

Bosphorus Strait: Cruise Options and Attractions

The Bosphorus Strait, a narrow natural strait that connects the Black Sea to the Sea of Marmara as well as forming part of the continental barrier between Europe and Asia, is one of Istanbul's most prominent geographical and cultural features. Along the Bosphorus, one can genuinely appreciate Istanbul's dynamic energy, a city that effortlessly bridges two continents.

From medieval mansions and fortresses to modern eateries and nightlife, the Bosphorus provides a unique glimpse into the heart of one of the world's most thriving cities. Cruising on the Bosphorus not only provides a new view of the city but also allows you to enjoy its breathtaking skyline and historic buildings.

Historical Significance of the Bosporus Strait

The Bosphorus' strategic importance has been recognized for millennia, with it serving as a critical gateway for successive empires such as the Roman, Byzantine, and Ottoman. Because of its dominance over the maritime route between the Mediterranean and the Black Sea, the strait has played host to numerous historical conflicts and discussions. Today, it is still an important canal for the maritime transit of goods, mainly oil and gas.

Explore the Bosphorus: Cruise Options.

Full Bosphorus Tour: A thorough trip of the Bosphorus Strait normally begins in Eminönü or Besiktas on the European side and continues to the Black Sea. This longer route allows passengers to observe the whole length of the strait, traveling beneath the famed Bosphorus Bridge and Fatih Sultan Mehmet Bridge. It also includes stops at major places such as Anadolu Kavağı, a popular spot near the Black Sea noted for its seafood eateries.

Short Circle Bosphorus Tours: These are shorter trips that provide a quick sight of the Bosphorus, perfect for those with limited time. They usually run approximately two hours and cover the principal attractions along the European and Asian coasts, up to the Second Bosphorus Bridge and back.

Sunset & Dinner Cruises: Sunset and supper cruises offer a more romantic experience. These cruises are ideal for taking in Istanbul's panoramic views at twilight, as well as great meals and, in many cases, live entertainment.

Private Yacht Tours: Private trips provide a more personalized experience on the Bosphorus. Visitors can charter sailboats for a personalized tour, generally accompanied by a guide who explains the historical and cultural value of the locations along the strait.

Night cruises: Night cruises on the Bosphorus provide a beautiful experience as city lights reflect on the river. These cruises frequently offer traditional

Turkish entertainment and dinner, highlighting Istanbul's lively nightlife.

Key attractions along the Bosphorus.

The Dolmabahçe Palace: This sumptuous house, located on the European coast of the Bosphorus, mixes classic Ottoman construction with European ornamental traditions, making it one of Istanbul's most spectacular palaces.

The Rumeli Fortress: Built by Mehmed the Conqueror in 1452, shortly before the conquest of Constantinople, this stronghold provides a panoramic view of the strait and serves as a museum and cultural venue.

Maiden's Tower (Kız Kulesi): The Maiden's Tower, perched on a small islet near the southern entrance of the Bosphorus, is one of Istanbul's most distinctive structures, with a rich history and tales.

The Beylerbeyi Palace: Built-in the 1860s, this imperial Ottoman summer palace is located on the Asian side of the Bosphorus. It is known for its beautiful blend of Western and Eastern architectural elements.

Ortaköy Mosque: This lovely mosque, located directly by the river near the Bosphorus Bridge, is one of Istanbul's most gorgeous surroundings, embodying a spectacular example of Neo-Baroque architecture.

Tips For Bosphorus Cruises

Booking in Advance: To reserve a space on a cruise, book ahead of time, especially during peak tourist seasons.

Weather Considerations: Check the weather forecast before embarking on a cruise, since clear, calm days may make the experience more enjoyable.

Cultural observation: When disembarking at different destinations, dress modestly and observe local customs to improve interactions with local communities.

Safety Measures: Always follow the safety precautions presented on the tour, especially on smaller or private boats.

A Bosphorus cruise is a unique and fascinating way to experience Istanbul, presenting a new view of the city that cannot be obtained on land. Whether you choose a brief tour, a sumptuous dinner cruise, or a private yacht expedition, the Bosphorus Strait is sure to provide spectacular views and a refreshing glimpse into Istanbul's character. As you fly between continents, you'll see not only the intersection of East and West but also the eternal beauty that has made Istanbul a crossroads of civilizations for ages.

Basilica Cistern: The Sunken Palace.

The Basilica Cistern, located deep beneath Istanbul's streets, is one of the city's most fascinating historical sites. The ancient cistern, also known as "Yerebatan Sarayı" or "The Sunken Palace," is an architectural marvel that demonstrates the Byzantine Empire's ingenuity and vision.

The Basilica Cistern, built in the sixth century by Emperor Justinian I, is the largest of several hundred ancient cisterns beneath the city. Today, it is not only a tribute to old Constantinople's historical and mechanical skills but also a must-see destination for tourists interested in Istanbul's rich history.

Historical significance.

The Basilica Cistern was built in 532 AD to provide water for the Great Palace and other buildings on Constantinople's First Hill. It was built to filter water for Byzantine emperors and delivered via aqueducts from a reservoir near the Black Sea, demonstrating the city's excellent municipal infrastructure. The cistern is an essential reminder of the Byzantines' capacity to adapt to the city's growing population and the need for a consistent water supply, particularly during the city's repeated sieges throughout history.

An architectural marvel.

The Basilica Cistern, which covers an area of around 9,800 square meters, can retain 80,000 cubic meters of water. The ceiling is supported by a forest of 336 marble columns, each 9 meters tall and organized into 12 rows of 28 columns each. These columns are a blend of Ionic, Doric, and Corinthian forms, frequently recycled from previous buildings, and demonstrate the Roman practice of spolia. The symmetry and sheer grandeur of the column arrangement create a surreal environment that captivates visitors.

The two Medusa head sculptures in the cistern's northwest corner, which serve as supports for two columns, are perhaps its most recognized feature. These skulls' provenance is unknown, however, they are assumed to have come from a late Roman edifice. They are arranged with one head sideways and the other upside down, which is said to nullify the power of Gorgon's gaze, a popular technique throughout the Roman period.

Explore the Basilica Cistern.

Visitors to the Basilica Cistern enter through a modest building on Sultanahmet Square and descend a 52-step stone staircase to the cold, dimly illuminated room below. Once inside, wooden pathways perched over the shallow waters lead guests through the huge, gloomy interior. The cistern is frequently illuminated with gentle, orange illumination that reflects off the water and columns, creating a tranquil and slightly creepy environment that feels like going back in time.

The air inside the cistern is chilly and damp, providing a pleasant relief from Istanbul's sweltering summers. The sound of trickling water resonates through the columns, adding to the mysterious atmosphere in the cistern. This ambiance is periodically accompanied by classical music, which is played to improve the tourist experience and the cistern's acoustic qualities.

The Cistern Today

In recent years, the Basilica Cistern has undergone many renovations to preserve its structural integrity and historical significance. Its distinctive ambiance and acoustics make it a popular site for cultural events like concerts and art exhibitions, in addition to being a tourist destination. The cistern has also appeared in several novels and films, most notably Dan Brown's "Inferno" and the James Bond film "From Russia with Love," which have helped to increase its reputation.

Visitors frequently conclude their trip by reflecting on the ancient Romans' incredible engineering talents and the ongoing need to maintain such historical buildings. The Basilica Cistern, with its rich history, architectural beauty, and cultural significance, is a powerful reminder of Istanbul's ability to retain its past while thriving as a vibrant modern metropolis.

The Basilica Cistern is more than just a historic storage facility; it represents innovation and perseverance. This "Sunken Palace" provides a rare view into the Byzantine Empire's creativity, as well as a reminder of previous civilizations' skilled urban planning and resource management.

A visit to the Basilica Cistern is a journey into the past, an investigation of the silent, watery ruins that once vibrated with life, supporting one of the most powerful cities in the ancient world. The experience of wandering the wooden walks between the columns, illuminated by dim light reflecting off the tranquil waters, is nothing short of amazing.

Galata Tower: Panoramic Views and History

Perched magnificently above Istanbul's skyline, the Galata Tower provides some of the most breathtaking views of the city, covering the Golden Horn, the Bosphorus, and the historical peninsula. Aside from its purpose as a famous perspective, the tower is rich in history, serving as a tribute to Istanbul's architectural prowess and stormy past. From its erection as a watchtower in the 14th century to its current prominence as a cultural and tourist destination, the Galata Tower has observed and survived many of the city's most significant events.

Historical Background.

The Galata Tower, originally known as Christea Turris (Tower of Christ) by the Genoese, was constructed in 1348 amid an expansion of the Genoese colony in Constantinople. It was part of a larger fortification effort, acting as a watchtower and marker for the Genoese fortified colony. The tower's strategic location gave it control over the harbor and the commercial activity that flowed through the region, which was once a thriving trade center outside the Byzantine fortifications.

The tower has served a variety of purposes throughout the centuries. During the Ottoman Empire, it acted as a fire watchtower, assisting in the detection and management of regular fires that threatened Istanbul's predominantly wooden architecture. It has also served as a prison, and a naval store, and was even repurposed into an observatory. Its purpose and functions have evolved to meet the demands and events of each era, resulting in a dynamic and enduring symbol of Istanbul.

Architectural Features

The Galata Tower, at roughly 67 meters (220 feet) tall, dominates the Galata skyline. It is a cylindrical stone tower made primarily of limestone and topped with a conical roof that has been rebuilt multiple times throughout history, most notably following earthquake damage. The tower's interior consists of several wooden floors connected by a spiral staircase that spirals around the tower's inner wall.

The upper half features a 360-degree viewing gallery that offers tourists unrivaled panoramic views of Istanbul's most renowned sights, such as the Hagia Sophia, Topkapi Palace, and the Bosphorus Bridge. The structure's design and capacity to provide such commanding views of the cityscape have made it a long-standing tourist attraction and a focus point for photographers and amorous visitors alike.

Panoramic Views and Their Impact

The view from the top of the Galata Tower is undoubtedly its most important attraction. Visitors are treated to a visual feast that includes the old city of Istanbul, modern areas, and the bustling canals that separate the city from Asia and Europe. The ability to see the city from such a height provides not only excellent photo opportunities but also a unique perspective on Istanbul's geographical shape and historical expansion.

During the day, the panoramas are clear, allowing for precise views of distant sites, while at night, the city lights provide a stunning display. The tower's top deck is frequently recognized as one of the greatest sites in Istanbul to watch the sunset, as the sun sinks below the horizon, casting golden hues throughout the city.

Cultural Significance

Today, the Galata Tower is more than just a historical landmark; it is an active component of Istanbul's cultural landscape. On the higher floors of the tower, there is a restaurant and café that serves traditional Turkish food as well as beautiful views. On the nights, the tower transforms to the sounds of Turkish music and dance performances, giving tourists a taste of Turkish cultural heritage.

The tower is also a focal point for local festivals and a popular location for both local and foreign films and television programs, reinforcing its role as Istanbul's cultural ambassador.

Preserving History

Preservation efforts have been vital to preserve the Galata Tower's structural integrity and historical correctness. These measures ensure that the tower can resist the natural elements as well as the wear and tear that comes with hosting hundreds of thousands of visitors each year. Recent restorations and upgrades to its facilities aim to improve the visitor experience while conserving the tower's historical character.

The Galata Tower is more than just a stone-and-mortar construction; it is a living museum that sheds light on Istanbul's rich past. It serves as a beacon for travelers, historians, and anyone drawn to the appeal of seeing a modern metropolis through the lens of history. The sensation of ascending the old spiral staircase to the noises of the city below and emerging to the panoramic splendor of Istanbul is both timeless and transformative, connecting the history and present of this ever-changing city. For everyone visiting Istanbul, the Galata Tower is a striking reminder of the city's eternal beauty and historical significance.

Dolmabahçe Palace: A Blend of European and Ottoman Architectures

Dolmabahçe Palace, with its majestic façade reaching down the Bosphorus in Istanbul, is more than just a palace; it represents Turkey's embrace of Westernisation in the mid-nineteenth century while preserving the Ottoman Empire's sumptuous traditions. This stately palace not only exhibits a distinct blend of European and Ottoman architectural characteristics, but it also represents a crucial shift in the cultural and political landscape of the Ottoman Empire as it transitions into modern Turkey.

History of the Dolmabahçe Palace

Dolmabahçe Palace, erected between 1843 and 1856 under Sultan Abdülmecid I's reign, replaced the old Topkapı Palace to meet the needs of a modern empire. Architects Garabet Balyan and his son Nigoğayos Balyan, from the famed Balyan family, were commissioned by the Sultan to design several notable projects in Istanbul during the 19th century.

Dolmabahçe's building signaled a break from conventional Ottoman palace design, combining considerable European elements, including Baroque, Rococo, and Neoclassical while retaining traditional Ottoman architecture.

Architectural grandeur

Dolmabahçe Palace is one of Turkey's largest palaces, with 285 rooms, 44 halls, 68 toilets, and 6 Turkish baths spread across 45,000 square meters. The palace's design reflects the Ottoman Empire's grandeur and vision in its closing years.

Exterior Design: The palace's exterior combines classical Western forms with traditional Ottoman elements like fluid calligraphy and floral motifs. The palace's main façade overlooks the sea and features a long row of elegant windows and balconies, emphasizing the Bosphorus' strategic and aesthetic value in Ottoman urban design.

Interior Decoration: The interior of Dolmabahçe Palace is as extravagant as its appearance, with an abundance of gold, crystal, and marble. The palace contains one of the world's largest Bohemian crystal chandeliers, a gift from Queen Victoria that weighs 4.5 tonnes and hangs in the ceremonial hall. The floors are covered in Hereke rugs, and the ceilings are adorned with murals that combine Islamic art elements with Baroque and Rococo designs.

The Ceremonial Hall (Muayede Salonu): is the most well-known chamber, and it is utilized for significant state occasions and receptions. It has a large dome that rises 36 meters high, which is highlighted by a big crystal chandelier.

Cultural Significance

Dolmabahçe Palace is not only a popular tourist site but also a cultural landmark that connects Turkey's historical story from the Ottoman Empire to today's republic. The palace was the empire's administrative center before becoming the presidential house of Mustafa Kemal Atatürk, the founder of modern Turkey. Atatürk spent his final days in the palace, where he died on November 10, 1938. The clock in his bedroom is famously set to the time of his death, 9:05 a.m., commemorating a painful event in Turkish history.

Visiting the Dolmabahçe Palace

Dolmabahçe Palace is now open to the public as a museum, with guided tours exploring its rich history, architecture, and the legacy of those who lived there. Visitors can stroll through its lush gardens, enjoy the meticulous design of its interiors, and learn about the lives of the last Ottoman sultans and the early years of the Turkish Republic.

What To Expect:

Visitors should plan for a visual feast. Each section of the palace, from the harem to the ceremonial halls, tells a unique story, not only about the architectural trends of the time but also about Sultan Abdülmecid I's personal tastes and political ambitions. The palace's setting along the Bosphorus provides a picturesque backdrop, ideal for photographs that capture the essence of Istanbul's imperial past mixed with its cosmopolitan present.

Dolmabahçe Palace is a marvel of its day, capturing the Ottoman Empire's splendor and forward-thinking ambition. It stands as a memorial to an empire at the crossroads of East and West, combining both architectural and artistic traditions to produce something unique to Turkey. A visit to Dolmabahçe Palace provides a comprehensive understanding of Istanbul's cultural and historical growth, as well as the aesthetic and political transformations that have created this lively metropolis.

Suleymaniye Mosque: An Architectural Marvel

The Suleymaniye Mosque, perched atop one of Istanbul's seven hills, is not only an important religious site but also a symbol of Ottoman architectural and artistic grandeur. The mosque, designed by famed architect Mimar Sinan for Sultan Suleiman the Magnificent, was built between 1550 and 1557.

It exemplifies the expertise of Ottoman engineering in the 16th century, as well as the aesthetic vision that characterized Suleiman's rule, also known as the Ottoman Empire's Golden Age. This architectural marvel flawlessly combines spiritual grace and grandeur, making it one of Istanbul's most popular historical attractions.

Historical significance.

Sultan Suleiman envisioned the Suleymaniye Mosque as a great undertaking to commemorate his rule and the Ottoman Empire's apex. The mosque not only serves religious reasons, but it also houses schools, a library, a hospital, a kitchen, and baths, exemplifying the Ottoman tradition of constructing külliyes, or community service complexes. The choice of Mimar Sinan, the empire's leading architect, to design the mosque ensured that it would be an architectural marvel unsurpassed in the empire's history.

Sinan, who was almost 70 years old when he started construction on the Suleymaniye, used all of his previous project experience, hoping to outdo the scale and splendor of the Hagia Sophia, the city's peak of Byzantine architecture. The end product was a mosque that exemplified Ottoman construction aspirations and capabilities while also demonstrating innovative engineering solutions.

Architectural Features

Domes and minarets: The main dome of the Suleymaniye Mosque is 53 meters tall and has a diameter of 27.25 meters. It is supported by four enormous piers and two partial domes. The dome is a breathtaking sight, displaying Sinan's talent for reaching new architectural heights. The mosque is flanked by four minarets, indicating that Suleiman was the fourth Ottoman sultan to rule following the conquest of Constantinople. The two higher minarets, standing at more than 70 meters each, are among the city's tallest.

Interior Design: The mosque's interior is a vast area illuminated by 249 stained-glass windows, which add to the aura of divine lighting. The interior design features Iznik tiles, calligraphy by Hasan Çelebi, and natural light, creating an awe-inspiring and welcoming atmosphere. The mihrab and minbar are finely carved from marble, and the prayer hall is large enough to accommodate thousands of worshippers.

Acoustics: The acoustic design is one of Sinan's most notable contributions to the Suleymaniye Mosque. The mosque is structured such that sound waves penetrate properly to every corner of the enormous room, due to carefully placed hollow pottery jars in the walls and beneath the dome. This idea demonstrates Sinan's insight in combining usefulness and aesthetic components.

External structures and courtyards: The mosque complex features a huge courtyard enclosed by an arcade of columns and arches, which is typical of Ottoman mosque architecture. This outside courtyard, with an ablution fountain in the center, gives a peaceful spot for reflection before entering the main prayer area. The mosque's overall symmetry, along with its auxiliary buildings, adds to a sense of balance and harmony that complements the structure's spiritual function.

Cultural and artistic significance

The Suleymaniye Mosque is a cultural beacon that has survived centuries of history, including countless earthquakes and fires that have ravaged Istanbul throughout the years. It not only symbolizes Ottoman religious commitment, but it also represents the creative and intellectual pursuits that flourished under Suleiman's rule.

The mosque's library housed a collection of rare manuscripts and served as a learning center, attracting intellectuals from all across the empire. The connected social complex, which featured a hospital, a soup kitchen, and an educational institution, demonstrated the Ottoman dedication to social welfare and community service.

Visiting the Suleymaniye Mosque.

The mosque provides tourists with a quiet and meditative atmosphere, in contrast to the hectic activity found on Istanbul's streets. The graves of Sultan Suleiman and his wife Hurrem Sultan, which are located beside the mosque in a wonderfully decorated tomb, add to the historical significance of the visit. Tourists are recommended to visit during non-prayer times and to dress modestly to show respect for this hallowed area.

The Suleymaniye Mosque, with its imposing dome, graceful minarets, and harmonious interior, represents the pinnacle of Ottoman architectural achievement. It captures the spiritual, cultural, and creative atmosphere of what is regarded as the Ottoman Empire's golden age. A visit to the Suleymaniye Mosque in Istanbul is more than just a historical tour; it is also an encounter with a masterpiece of human creation and dedication. As a result, this mosque is not only an important site of prayer but also a symbol of one of history's most powerful empires.

Istanbul Archaeology Museums: A Treasure Trove

Tucked away in the heart of Istanbul, the Istanbul Archaeology Museums complex is a hidden jewel that takes visitors on a journey through time, revealing the rich and diverse history of civilizations that have left their mark on this historic city.

This complex, which includes three main museums—the Archaeological Museum, the Museum of the Ancient Orient, and the Tiled Kiosk Museum—houses over a million artifacts from numerous cultures dating back thousands of years. The museums offer a comprehensive view of the region's historical and cultural history, from the earliest human settlements to the splendor of the Ottoman Empire.

Historical Background.

The Istanbul Archaeology Museums were founded in the late nineteenth century, mostly via the efforts of

Osman Hamdi Bey, a pioneering figure in Turkish archaeology and museology. Hamdi Bey's ambition was to establish a museum that would preserve and make historical artifacts from the Ottoman Empire available to visitors. The Archaeological Museum debuted in 1891 and was followed by the Museum of the Ancient Orient and the Tiled Kiosk Museum. The founding of these museums was a crucial step towards the preservation and study of Turkey's rich ancient legacy.

The Archaeological Museum

The Archaeological Museum, the largest of the three, houses a wealth of artifacts that document the history of the ancient Near East, Anatolia, and the wider Mediterranean region. Its collection is organized thematically and chronologically, providing visitors with a thorough perspective of human history.

Highlights from the Collection

The Alexander Sarcophagus: One of the most well-known displays is the Alexander Sarcophagus, a beautiful piece that was incorrectly thought to belong to Alexander the Great. It is a superb example of Hellenistic art, carved from marble and embellished with exquisite bas-reliefs representing scenes from Alexander's fight and hunting.

The Sidamara Sarcophagus: The Sidamara Sarcophagus is a huge Roman sarcophagus from the third century AD that is known for its ornate carvings and high-quality craftsmanship.

The Treaty of Kadesh: This ancient clay tablet, considered the oldest known peace treaty, documents the agreement between the Egyptians and the Hittites following the Battle of Kadesh in 1274 BC.

The Sumerian Tablets: These tablets shed light on the daily lives, judicial institutions, and economic activities of the Sumerians, one of the earliest known civilizations.

The Museum of Ancient Orient

The Museum of the Ancient Orient, which is situated in an Alexandre Vallaury-designed building, displays artifacts from Anatolia, Mesopotamia, Egypt, and the Arabian Peninsula before Islam. This museum focuses on the significant cultural interactions between these ancient civilizations.

Key Exhibits:

The Ishtar Gate: Fragments of Babylon's magnificent gate are on exhibit, providing a look into the majesty of Mesopotamian architecture.

The Kadesh pact: The museum also contains a different version of this historic pact, emphasizing its importance in ancient times.

Egyptian Mummies and Sarcophagi: These exhibits offer insight into ancient Egypt's funerary rituals and beliefs.

Hittite Artifacts: Statues, reliefs, and inscriptions shed light on the Hittite civilization, which played an important role in Anatolia's history.

The Tiled Kiosk Museum

The Tiled Kiosk Museum, also known as "Çinili Köşk," was commissioned by Sultan Mehmed II in 1472 and is one of the oldest remaining structures in the complex. The museum's architecture is a combination of Seljuk and Ottoman styles, making it a visually appealing exhibit in its own right. The museum specializes in Islamic art and has a large collection of ceramics and tiles from the Seljuk and Ottoman periods.

Notable displays:

Iznik Tiles: Known for their brilliant colors and elaborate designs, these tiles are among the finest specimens of Ottoman porcelain art.

Ceramics from Kütahya and Çanakkale: The museum showcases ceramics from Kütahya and

Çanakkale, which were famed for their manufacturing. The items are historically significant and attractive.

Seljuk Artifacts: Seljuk artifacts include architectural features and common things that shed light on the Seljuks' artistic traditions and daily lives.

Educational and Cultural Impact

The Istanbul Archaeology Museums are not just repositories for historical artifacts, but also teaching centers that encourage the study and enjoyment of archaeology and history. The museums provide a variety of educational programs, such as talks, workshops, and guided tours, to interest visitors of all ages. These programs provide to a better understanding of the historical background and cultural importance of the artifacts on show.

Modern Facilities and Renovations

Over the years, the museums have undergone numerous modifications to improve the tourist experience. Climate-controlled galleries, interactive displays, and new lighting have been added to protect the preservation of the artifacts while also providing visitors with a more interesting and educational experience.

In recent years, museums have embraced digital technology, providing virtual tours and online exhibits that let visitors from all over the world study their holdings. These initiatives have served to improve the museums' accessibility and reach, allowing them to share their unique treasures with a global audience.

Visiting the museums

Visitors to the Istanbul Archaeology Museums should plan on spending a whole day exploring the rich collections. The museums are in the Eminönü district, close to other significant sights including Topkapi Palace and the Hagia Sophia, making them easily integrated into a larger itinerary of Istanbul's historical landmarks.

Tip for Visitors:

Purchase Tickets in Advance: To avoid long lines, particularly during busy tourist seasons.

Join a Guided Tour: To gain a better knowledge of the artifacts and their historical contexts.

Wear comfortable shoes: as the museum complex is large and requires a lot of walking.

Take Breaks: Museums have cafés where visitors can relax and enjoy refreshments while pondering on the exhibits.

The Istanbul Archaeology Museums are a witness to Istanbul's and the neighboring regions' rich and diverse histories. Through their enormous collections and interesting displays, they provide a unique glimpse into the past civilizations that have created this intriguing city. Whether you are a history buff, an archaeologist, or simply a curious traveler, a visit to these museums promises to be both gratifying and educational. The artifacts stored within its walls not only narrate the history of Istanbul but also emphasize the significance of maintaining and understanding our common human legacy.

Parks and Outdoor Activities in Istanbul

Istanbul, a city that perfectly merges the ancient and modern, has a variety of parks and outdoor activities ideal for families seeking adventure, leisure, and cultural enrichment. The city's parks offer green places for picnicking, playing, and exploring, while a variety of outdoor activities cater to families seeking to enjoy the city's natural beauty and lively environment. This guide explores Istanbul's top parks and outdoor activities, focusing on family-friendly alternatives that make the city an ideal vacation for both parents and children.

Explore Istanbul's Parks.

Gülhane Park: Gülhane Park, located on Istanbul's ancient peninsula and near Topkapi Palace, is one of the city's oldest and most prominent parks. It was originally part of the palace grounds and became open to the public in 1912. The park is well-known for its lovely gardens, walking lanes, and stunning views of the Bosphorus. Families can enjoy strolls, picnics, and playgrounds in the park. The Istanbul Museum of the History of Science and Technology in Islam, located in the park, provides an educational experience through exhibits that highlight Islamic scientific achievements.

Emirgan Park: Emirgan Park, located along the Bosphorus in the Emirgan neighborhood, is well-known for its tulip gardens, particularly during the Istanbul Tulip Festival in April. The park spans 117 acres and has three historic pavilions, wide walking routes, playgrounds, and picnic spots. Families can spend the day exploring the colorful flowerbeds, enjoying the open areas, and stopping by the park's café for refreshments.

Yildiz Park: Yildiz Park, located between Beşiktaş and Ortaköy, provides a relaxing respite with its lush foliage, decorative ponds, and historical pavilions. The park was once part of the imperial hunting grounds, but it is now a pleasant getaway for both locals and tourists. The park's large grounds are perfect for family picnics, natural hikes, and exploring the Yildiz Palace complex, including the stunning Malta and Çadır pavilions.

Fethi Paşa Koruşu: Fethi Paşa Korusu, located on Istanbul's Asian side, overlooks the Bosphorus and offers stunning views of the city in a serene setting. The park has walking pathways, picnic areas, and playgrounds. Its elevation location makes it an ideal spot for families to spend a relaxing day outside, with the added benefit of panoramic views of Istanbul's skyline.

Belgrade Forest: For families looking for a more adventurous outdoor experience, Belgrad Forest, located on the outskirts of Istanbul, has huge woodlands and trails ideal for hiking, bicycling, and picnics. The forest is a favorite weekend getaway destination, offering a natural break from the rush and bustle of city life. Belgrad Forest, with its designated picnic sites, ponds, and diverse flora and fauna, is an ideal location for nature-loving families.

Outdoor Activities for Families

Bosphorus Cruise: A Bosphorus cruise is the quintessential Istanbul experience, providing families with a unique view of the city's monuments from the water. There are a variety of cruise options available, including short outings and full-day excursions. Families may enjoy the panoramic splendor of the Bosphorus while passing by famous landmarks including the Dolmabahçe Palace, Rumeli Fortress, and Maiden's Tower. Many cruises have eating options, making it an enjoyable way to spend an afternoon or evening.

Prince's Islands: The Princes' Islands, located just a short ferry journey from Istanbul, are a popular family day trip destination. Büyükada, the largest island, is car-free, allowing families to explore by bike or horse-drawn carriage. The islands have beaches, old homes, and verdant parks. Families can have fun swimming, picnicking, and visiting the lovely streets and local cafes.

Miniaturk: Miniaturk, a tiny park on the Golden Horn, showcases scale miniatures of Turkey's most iconic sights and historical locations. The park is an instructive and exciting experience for both children and adults, providing an opportunity to learn about Turkey's rich history. Miniaturk, with over 120 models, interactive exhibitions, and a playground, offers families a fun and educational visit.

Istanbul Aquarium: Istanbul Aquarium, located in Florya, is one of the world's largest thematic aquariums. It provides an immersive experience through themed parts reflecting various regions of the world's oceans and seas. Families may learn about a variety of marine life, including tropical fish and sharks, and participate in interactive exhibits. The aquarium also has a 5D cinema, making it a fascinating place for kids.

Vialand (Işfanbul): For families looking for a day of excitement and amusement, Vialand, now known as Istanbul, is Istanbul's leading theme park. Istanbul, located in the Eyüp district, offers a variety of rides and attractions for all ages, including roller coasters and water rides. The park also offers shopping, food, and entertainment, offering a fun-filled day for the entire family.

Parks with playgrounds: Istanbul has various parks with modern playgrounds where children may enjoy safe outside play. Notable examples include Maçka Park in Şişli, Bebek Park in Beşiktaş, and Moda Park in Kadıköy. These parks offer plenty of areas for children to run, play, and engage with one another, while parents can unwind and enjoy the scenery.

Hikes & Nature Walks: For families who enjoy hiking and exploring nature, Istanbul has various paths and parks that offer a refreshing outdoor experience. Polonezköy Nature Park, located on the Asian side, offers well-marked trails, picnic spots, and the opportunity to explore the region's natural splendor. Another excellent choice is the Aydos Forest, which has hiking routes and gorgeous views that are ideal for a family day out.

Beach outings: During the warmer months, Istanbul's beaches are popular destinations for family trips. Florya Beach, near the Istanbul Aquarium, and Caddebostan Beach, on the Asian side, have sandy beaches, swimming places, and picnic and relaxing spots. These beaches offer an excellent opportunity for families to enjoy the sun, water, and sand without leaving the city.

Educational and Cultural Activities.

The Rahmi M. Koç Museum: This industrial museum, located on the banks of the Golden Horn, provides an intriguing glimpse into the history of transportation, manufacturing, and communication. The museum's interactive exhibits, which include historic cars, trains, and airplanes, provide an exciting and instructive experience for children. The museum also has a playground, a submarine tour, and a ferryboat, offering a fun and educational visit for the entire family.

Istanbul Toy Museum: Founded by Turkish poet and author Sunay Akın, the Istanbul Toy Museum in Kadıköy houses a diverse collection of toys from various eras and nations. The museum is set in a historic mansion and contains displays that will appeal to both children and adults. It takes visitors on a nostalgic trip through toy history while also providing educational information on cultural and historical settings.

Children's Science Centres: Istanbul features various science centers with interactive and instructive exhibits for children. The Istanbul Museum of the History of Science and Technology in Islam, located in Gülhane Park, explains how Muslim intellectuals advanced science. The Istanbul Aquarium is another outstanding site that blends marine biology and experiential learning.

Seasonal and Special Events.

Tulip Festival: Every April, the Istanbul Tulip Festival commemorates the city's historical link to tulips, which are endemic to Turkey. During the event, parks such as Emirgan Park and Gülhane Park are decorated with millions of flowering tulips, resulting in a breathtaking visual show. The festival offers a variety of activities, music, and cultural events, making it a great time for families to come and enjoy the lively environment.

Ramadan festivities: During the holy month of Ramadan, Istanbul's parks and squares are filled with special events, nightly markets, and cultural performances. Families may immerse themselves in the festive mood by visiting places like Sultanahmet Square, where traditional food booths, entertainment, and community iftar dinners provide a one-of-a-kind and unforgettable experience.

Istanbul's parks and outdoor activities provide a varied choice of family-friendly options to suit all interests and ages. Every family may find something to enjoy, from touring lush gardens and historic places to participating in educational and cultural activities. The city's blend of natural beauty, rich

112

history, and vibrant culture allows families to make memorable memories while experiencing the finest of Istanbul. Whether you're planning a picnic in a picturesque park, a day of adventure at a theme park, or a cultural visit to a museum, Istanbul is the ideal setting for family fun and exploration.

Shopping in Istanbul: Bazaars and Modern Malls

Istanbul, which has been at the crossroads of civilizations for centuries, provides a vibrant and diversified shopping experience that perfectly blends the ancient with the new. From the convoluted lanes of ancient bazaars to the clean, modern bounds of luxury shopping malls, Istanbul has something for everyone's taste and budget. This tour delves into Istanbul's rich tapestry of shopping choices, highlighting the city's famous bazaars and modern malls for a unique shopping experience.

The Grand Bazaar

The Grand Bazaar, also known as Kapalıçarşı, is among the world's oldest and largest covered markets. Sultan Mehmed II founded the Grand Bazaar in the 15th century, and it is now a huge maze of over 60 alleyways and over 4,000 stores. It is a site where history, culture, and business meet, providing an unrivaled shopping experience

What To Buy:

Jewellery: The Grand Bazaar is well-known for its vast variety of gold, silver, and gemstone jewelry. Many of the pieces are handcrafted by talented artisans, making them distinctive mementos or gifts.

Carpets and Kilims: Turkish carpets and kilims are world-renowned for their quality and craftsmanship. The bazaar offers a wide range of designs, from classic to contemporary, to suit all tastes.

Ceramics: The exquisite designs of Turkish ceramics reflect the country's rich creative tradition. Look for colorful tiles, plates, and bowls with traditional Ottoman and Anatolian themes.

Spices & drinks: The bazaar is a sensory experience, with stalls selling a wide range of spices and drinks. From saffron and sumac to apple tea and Turkish pleasure, these things make great culinary gifts.

Textiles and Leather Goods: The Grand Bazaar is a treasure trove for textiles and leather goods. Scarves, shawls, and leather coats are popular purchases that showcase the best Turkish craftsmanship.

Tips for Shopping:

Bargaining: Haggling is widespread in the Grand Bazaar. Begin by offering half the asking price and negotiating from there. It's all part of the experience, so enjoy it.

Explore: Take your time exploring the bazaar's numerous lanes and shops. Some of the better finds are off the main thoroughfares.

Stay Alert: The Grand Bazaar can get crowded, so keep a watch on your possessions and be aware of your surroundings.

The Spice Bazaar: A feast for the senses.

The Spice Bazaar, also known as the Egyptian Bazaar (Mısır Çarşısı), is a small yet interesting market located in the Eminönü area. It was built in the 17th century and served as a spice trading hub.

What To Buy:

Spices: The Spice Bazaar lives true to its name with a variety of spices that will enrich your culinary creativity. Look for aromatic combinations such as baharat, sumac, and paprika.

Dried Fruits and Nuts: The bazaar sells a range of dried fruits and nuts, including apricots, figs, and pistachios, which are ideal for a nutritious snack or as gifts.

Turkish delight (lokum) and baklava are must-try desserts. Many stalls offer samples, allowing you to try before you buy.

Herbal Teas: From classic Turkish tea to herbal blends, the Spice Bazaar has a large range to pick from.

Tips for Shopping

Samples: Do not be afraid to ask for samples, especially of spices and sweets. Vendors are usually willing to let you try their products.

Freshness: Make sure that the things you purchase, particularly spices and teas, are fresh and properly wrapped.

Modern Malls: Contemporary Shopping in Istanbul.

While Istanbul's bazaars provide an insight into the city's rich history, its modern malls represent its bustling present and future. These malls offer a premium shopping experience with worldwide brands, high-end apparel, and a wide range of restaurants and entertainment options.

Isinye Park: Istinye Park, located in Istanbul's Sarıyer district, is a popular shopping destination. The mall houses a combination of high-end luxury labels such as Louis Vuitton, Chanel, and Dior, as well as renowned worldwide merchants like Zara and H&M. Istinye Park also has an open-air part with stores and cafes, providing a pleasant shopping environment.

Zorlu Centre: Zorlu Centre, located in the Beşiktaşdistrict, is more than a mall; it is a lifestyle complex. It features designer retailers such as Prada,

Gucci, and Fendi, as well as a cutting-edge performing arts center. The center's culinary options span from fine dining restaurants to trendy cafes, making it an ideal destination for a day out.

Kanyon Mall: Kanyon Mall, located in Levent, is well-known for its distinctive architectural design, which incorporates an open-air layout. The mall features a mix of luxury and high-street brands such as Harvey Nichols, Mango, and Nike. Kanyon also has several restaurants, a cinema, and a fitness center.

Cevahir Mall: Cevahir Mall, one of Europe's largest retail malls, is located in Şişli district. It has more than 300 stores, including both Turkish and foreign brands. The mall also includes a variety of dining options, a huge entertainment center a bowling alley, and a movie theatre.

Akmerkez: Akmerkez, located in Etiler, is an award-winning shopping mall that has served Istanbul since 1993. It features a mix of premium and mid-range companies, as well as several fine dining restaurants. The mall is noted for its exquisite architecture and excellent service.

Forum Istanbul: Forum Istanbul, located in the Bayrampaşa district, is one of Turkey's major shopping centers. It has a diverse assortment of stores, including fashion, electronics, and home items. The mall also houses many attractions, including an ice rink, a cinema, and the Istanbul Sea Life Aquarium.

Tips for Shopping at Malls

Sales & Discounts: Keep an eye out for sales, particularly throughout the summer and winter seasons. Many stores provide considerable discounts at these times.

Tax-Free Shopping: Non-EU travelers can enjoy tax-free shopping in Istanbul. Look for stores that provide tax-free services, and remember to save your receipts.

Dining and Entertainment: Maximise your shopping experience by exploring the malls' dining and entertainment options. Many malls provide high-quality restaurants, cafes, and entertainment facilities.

Street Markets and Local Bazaar

In addition to large bazaars and contemporary malls, Istanbul has many street markets and local bazaars that provide a more real shopping experience. These markets are excellent places to find fresh vegetables, local specialties, and one-of-a-kind handicrafts.

Kadıköy Market: Kadıköy Market, located on Istanbul's Asian side, is a bustling marketplace that sells a variety of fresh fruit, fish, spices, and more. It's a terrific place to learn about local cuisine and culture and pick up some unique ingredients for your kitchen.

Beşiktaş Market: The Beşiktaş Market, held every Saturday, is a popular local destination for fresh fruits and vegetables, apparel, and household items.

The market has a bustling atmosphere and is an excellent place to meet people and locate bargains.

Fatih Market: The Fatih Market, often called the Wednesday Market (Çarşamba Pazarı), is one of Istanbul's main street marketplaces. It sells everything, from fresh fruit and fabrics to gadgets and toys. The market extends across several streets and draws a diverse crowd of shoppers.

Arasta Bazar: Arasta Bazaar, located behind the Blue Mosque, is a smaller and less congested alternative to the Grand Bazaar. It specializes in traditional crafts like carpets, ceramics, and jewelry. The bazaar is a great place to get high-quality souvenirs and gifts.

Tips for Shopping at Street Markets

Cash is King: Many merchants at street markets prefer payment, so keep plenty of local currency on available.

Early Bird: Go to markets early in the day to avoid crowds and obtain the best assortment of products.

Bargaining: is a typical practice in street markets. Approach the situation with a polite demeanor, and don't be afraid to bargain for a better price.

Whether you're meandering through the medieval lanes of the Grand Bazaar, inhaling the fragrances of the Spice Bazaar, or enjoying the modern conveniences of Istanbul's opulent malls, the city provides a unique and engaging shopping experience.

Each market and mall represent a different aspect of Istanbul's vibrant culture, offering a unique perspective on the city's past and present. From traditional crafts and local delicacies to worldwide brands and luxury goods, Istanbul's shopping scene caters to every taste and budget. Accept the dynamic atmosphere, delight in the delectable offers, and bring home a piece of Istanbul's beauty and legacy.

Nightlife & Entertainment in Istanbul

Istanbul, a city that never sleeps, has a bustling and diversified nightlife and entertainment scene to match its rich past. From traditional Turkish music performances in ancient locations to modern nightclubs buzzing with the latest beats, the city has something for everyone. Whether you want to immerse yourself in Turkey's rich cultural heritage or dance the night away at a fashionable rooftop club, Istanbul provides wonderful evenings and experiences.

Traditional Turkish Entertainment

Whirling dervishes: The Whirling Dervishes event is one of Istanbul's most unique and mesmerizing cultural experiences. The ceremony, which originated with the Sufi mystic Rumi's teachings, is a type of meditation through dance. The Dervishes, draped in flowing white robes and tall hats, spin gracefully to the hypnotic rhythm of traditional music, providing both a spiritual and visually breathtaking spectacle. These ceremonies are often held at venues such as the Galata Mevlevi Museum and the Hodjapasha Cultural Centre, providing visitors with an in-depth look at Turkish spirituality and cultural traditions.

Turkish Night Shows: Turkish night shows are another opportunity to enjoy traditional entertainment. These presentations often include a mix of acts, such as folk dances from various regions of Turkey, belly dancing, and live music. The shows are typically held in restaurants or cultural centers and include a full dinner featuring traditional Turkish cuisine. This interactive experience offers tourists a night of cultural enrichment while eating wonderful meals.

Live Turkish Music: Istanbul has various venues where you may hear live Turkish music. Local musicians frequently perform at venues such as Ağaç Ev, a cozy café in Kadıköy, and Babylon, a renowned music club in Beyoğlu. These venues offer an intimate setting in which to hear music ranging from traditional Turkish folk to contemporary pop and rock.

Modern Nightlife

Rooftop bars: Istanbul's skyline is lined with rooftop bars that provide breathtaking views of the Bosphorus, the Golden Horn, and the city's most famous buildings. These bars are ideal for sipping cocktails while admiring panoramic views. Mikla, located above the Marmara Pera Hotel, has a refined environment and serves modern Anatolian cuisine. Another favorite is 360 Istanbul, which is famed for its 360-degree views, varied menu, and lively environment.

Nightclubs: For those eager to dance the night away, Istanbul's nightclubs provide an electrifying atmosphere. Reina, since gone, was one of the city's most recognizable nightclubs, attracting celebrities and worldwide DJs. Other popular clubs include Sortie, located near the Bosphorus, and Klein, which is recognized for its cutting-edge electronic music and avant-garde interior design. These clubs frequently hold live DJ performances and themed parties, assuring a memorable evening.

Jazz and blues: Jazz fans can discover a vibrant scene in Istanbul. Nardis Jazz Club, located near the Galata Tower, is a cozy venue that hosts nightly concerts by local and international jazz musicians. The Istanbul Jazz Centre in Ortaköy is another excellent place to hear live jazz music, with an attractive atmosphere and a menu of superb food and drinks. These locations provide a calm ambiance in which to enjoy high-quality music in an intimate setting.

Culinary delights.

Late Night Dining: Istanbul's cuisine scene is as vibrant as its nightlife, with plenty of late-night dining alternatives to fulfill your cravings. Asmalımescit Street in Beyoğlu is a busy area with meyhanes (traditional Turkish bars) and restaurants that stay open late. These businesses serve a diverse selection of foods, including mezes (small appetizers), fresh fish, and grilled meats, all complemented by raki, a typical Turkish drink.

Street Food: For a more relaxed atmosphere, Istanbul's street cuisine is a must-try. Istiklal Street and the surrounding area are packed with vendors selling delectable foods like döner kebabs, simit (sesame-covered bread rings), and midye dolma (stuffed mussels). These street meals are ideal for grabbing a fast bite while exploring the city's nightlife.

Fine Dining: If you prefer a more upmarket eating experience, Istanbul has various fine dining establishments that serve exquisite cuisine and provide excellent service. Mikla, as previously said, is one of the city's best restaurants, with an inventive menu and breathtaking vistas. Another wonderful option is Neolokal, which serves modern renditions of traditional Turkish meals in a chic environment. These restaurants offer the ideal start to a night out, with menus that accentuate the rich flavors of Turkish cuisine.

Cultural Venues and Performances

Theatres and Opera houses: Istanbul is home to several prominent theatres and opera houses that feature a wide range of acts, including classical music, opera, modern plays, and dance. The Istanbul State Opera and Ballet, located in the Atatürk Cultural Centre, presents world-class performances that appeal to both locals and tourists. The Süreyya Opera House in Kadıköy is a stunning location for opera and ballet performances.

Concerts and festivals: Throughout the year, Istanbul offers a variety of concerts and festivals to celebrate music, arts, and culture. The Istanbul Music Festival, held in June, is one of the city's most important events, featuring performances by renowned performers and orchestras. The Istanbul Jazz Festival, which takes place in the summer, brings together jazz performers from all over the world for a series of concerts at various venues throughout the city. These festivals offer an excellent opportunity to experience Istanbul's thriving cultural scene.

Cinema & Film Festivals: Istanbul has a rich cinematic legacy, with various historic cinemas and modern multiplexes showing a diverse selection of films. The Istanbul Film Festival, held in April, features a broad variety of international and Turkish films, attracting cinephiles from all over the world. Venues such as the Atlas Cinema on Istiklal Street and the Istanbul Modern Museum's cinema show both mainstream and independent films, providing a broad cinematic experience.

Alternative Nightlife

Bosphorus Cruise: A nocturnal cruise on the Bosphorus provides a one-of-a-kind nightlife experience. These excursions provide a magical way to view the city's lit sights, including the Bosphorus Bridge, Dolmabahçe Palace, and Maiden's Tower. Many cruises include meals and live entertainment, creating an unforgettable evening on the lake.

Hookah lounges: Hookah lounges, also known as nargiles, are a popular alternative for a relaxing evening in Istanbul. These lounges include a large assortment of flavored tobaccos and a comfortable ambiance where you can relax with friends. Popular hookah clubs include Erenler Nargile in Sultanahmet, which is recognized for its traditional setting and good service, and Nargilem Café in Tophane, which has a more modern ambiance.

Art Gallery and Exhibitions: For a more culturally enriching evening, Istanbul's art galleries and exhibitions offer an intriguing peek into the city's vibrant art scene. Contemporary Turkish and foreign artists are featured in frequent shows at galleries such as Istanbul Modern and Pera Museum. These places frequently remain open late, providing a sophisticated and inspirational alternative to the usual nightlife scene.

LGBTQ+ Nightlife: Istanbul has a thriving LGBTQ+ community, with various bars and clubs catering particularly to this demographic. Tekyön, located in Taksim, is a renowned LGBTQ+ nightclub with an exciting dance floor and a welcoming atmosphere. Another popular spot is Love Dance Point, which has themed nights and live DJ performances. These establishments offer a secure and friendly environment for LGBTQ+ individuals and their friends to spend the night out.

Safety Advice for Nightlife in Istanbul

Stay in Groups: It is always safer to go out in groups, especially if you are unfamiliar with the surroundings.

Use Licenced Taxis: For safe transport to and from your nightlife hotspots, use renowned taxi services or ride-sharing applications.

Keep Valuables Secure: Take care of your valuables and avoid carrying big amounts of cash or expensive objects.

Stay Hydrated and Eat Well: To maintain your energy levels throughout the night, drink plenty of water and eat nutritious foods.

Istanbul's nightlife and entertainment culture is as broad and vibrant as the city itself, with something for everyone. From traditional Turkish shows and live music to sophisticated nightclubs and exquisite restaurants, the city offers amazing nights of excitement, culture, and pleasure. Whether you're a history buff, a music lover, a foodie, or a partygoer, Istanbul's dynamic nightlife will captivate and delight you, making your evenings in this incredible city as unforgettable as your days. Embrace Istanbul's vitality after dark and discover why this city is known for its nightlife and entertainment.

Traditional Turkish Arts and Crafts

Turkey, which spans two continents and connects the East and West, has a rich tapestry of arts and crafts that have grown over the ages. Traditional Turkish arts and crafts, which draw on a variety of civilizational influences, reflect the Turkish people's cultural history and artistic inventiveness. From elaborate carpets and delicate pottery to exquisite calligraphy and vivid textiles, these art forms offer a glimpse into Turkey's rich history and strong cultural identity. This research digs into traditional Turkish arts and crafts, emphasizing their historical significance, distinctive techniques, and ongoing appeal.

Turkish Rugs and Kilims

Historical significance: Turkish carpets and kilims are among the most well-known and recognizable elements of Turkish art. These woven masterpieces date back to ancient times and were originally constructed by nomadic tribes for practical purposes such as floor coverings, wall hangings, and bedding. Over time, they became highly valued works of art, representing wealth, position, and cultural identity.

Techniques and Material: Carpet weaving is a multigenerational craft that requires precise methods. The process begins with the selection of high-quality wool, cotton, or silk, which is dyed with natural ingredients to produce rich, brilliant colors. The weavers then use handlooms to delicately knot the fibers into intricate designs. Each area in Turkey has its unique designs and characteristics. For example:

Hereke Carpets: Known for their excellent silk and wool weaving, Hereke carpets have complicated designs and are commonly used in palaces.

Konya Kilims: These flat-woven rugs have geometric shapes and vibrant colors that reflect the region's nomadic tradition.

Cultural Importance: Carpets and kilims are fundamental to Turkish culture, and they are frequently presented as gifts to commemorate significant life events like as marriages and births. They also act as keepsakes, preserving family stories and customs.

Turkish ceramics

Historical Background: Turkey's ceramic art legacy extends back to the 8th century, with important improvements throughout the Seljuk and Ottoman periods. Turkish ceramics reached its height during the 16th century in İznik, which became the epicenter of pottery manufacture.

Techniques and styles: Turkish ceramics are noted for their unique designs and brilliant colors. The creation process consists of various stages, including clay shape, glazing, and burning. The elaborate patterns are frequently influenced by nature, including motifs like flowers, leaves, and birds. Some major styles include:

İznik Ceramics: is known for producing high-quality quartz-based tiles and pottery in vibrant colors including cobalt blue, turquoise, and coral red.

Kütahya ceramics: are known for their brilliant and diverse color palettes, as well as exquisite floral and geometric motifs.

Modern Relevance: Today, Turkish ceramics are highly appreciated, with artists keeping old processes while introducing contemporary designs. They are often seen in mosques, castles, and residences, serving as both decorative and practical elements.

Turkish calligraphy

Historical Development: Calligraphy, also known as "Hat" in Turkish, holds a special position in Islamic art since the written word is seen to mirror divine beauty. Turkish calligraphy evolved from Arabic scripts, with notable contributions from Ottoman calligraphers such as Sheikh Hamdullah and Hafiz Osman.

Techniques & Tools: Calligraphy demands accuracy and talent. Calligraphers employ "kalam" reed pens and natural-based ink. The method entails mastering numerous scripts, including:

Thuluth: script, known for its massive and graceful curves, is widely utilized in architectural embellishments.

Naskh: is a smaller, more legible script used to write the Quran and other literature.

Cultural Significance: Calligraphy is more than just decorative; it is a method of spiritual expression. It adorns mosques, manuscripts, and official documents, playing an important part in Turkey's visual cultural heritage. Modern calligraphers are constantly innovating, combining old techniques with contemporary trends.

Turkish Ebru (Marbling)

Origins and evolution: Ebru, or paper marbling, is a traditional Turkish art style that originated in Central Asia, was brought to Anatolia by the Seljuks, and evolved further during the Ottoman Empire. Colorful designs are created on water and then transferred to paper.

Techniques and processes: The process of making ebru is both complex and exciting. Artisans use a tray filled with water mixed with a sticky substance known as "kitre." They then drop colors onto the water's surface and manipulate them with various implements to form patterns. After the design is completed, a sheet of paper is carefully placed on the water's surface to absorb the colors.

Application and Modern Uses: Originally employed for book covers and endpapers, ebru art has found new applications in modern design, including as fashion and interior decor. Classes are available in workshops and studios around Turkey, helping to preserve this historic art form.

Turkish jewellery

Historical Context: Jewelry-making in Turkey has a long history dating back to ancient civilizations including the Hittites, Phrygians, and Byzantines. The art genre flourished during the Ottoman Empire, with influences from numerous cultures adding to its richness.

Techniques and Design: Turkish jewelry is renowned for its elaborate patterns and use of precious metals and stones. Filigree, which involves twisting and soldering fine metal threads to form intricate designs, is very popular. Common materials include gold, silver, turquoise, and coral.

Cultural Significance: Jewellery is an important part of Turkish culture, representing wealth, rank, and personal achievements. Traditional ornaments like "sarmasik" (vine) bracelets and "tuğra" (sultan's signature) pendants are treasured heirlooms handed down through generations.

Turkish textiles

Weaving and embroidery: Textile manufacture is another important aspect of Turkish arts and crafts. Weaving and needlework have been done for ages, producing everything from casual apparel to sacred outfits. Turkish textile art features distinctive techniques such as "tel kırma" (wire breaking) and "oya" (lace creation).

Famous textiles: Bursa silk, known for its fineness, has been a staple of the Turkish textile industry since the Ottoman era.

Yemeni: These are traditional handwoven headscarves with colorful embroidery that are commonly worn by women in rural communities.

Modern adaptations: Today, Turkish textiles thrive as artists and designers incorporate ancient techniques into modern fashion and home decor.

Turkish textiles are popular locally and globally due to their vivid patterns and high-quality craftsmanship.

Turkish Metalwork

Historical Roots: Metalworking is an ancient craft in Turkey, dating back to the Bronze Age. During the Ottoman Empire, metalwork reached new heights, with artists crafting elaborate objects for both everyday use and ornamentation.

Techniques and styles: Turkish metalwork employs a range of techniques, including engraving, filigree, and repoussé (hammered relief). Copper, brass, and silver are widely utilized materials. Items like coffee sets, trays, and ornamental plates demonstrate the artists' expertise and ingenuity.

Cultural Impact: Metalwork objects are commonly utilized in everyday life, ranging from tea service to home décor. They are also popular gifts that reflect Turkey's rich cultural past.

Turkish Shadow Puppetry (Karagöz, Hacivat)

Origins and history: Karagöz and Hacivat are classic Turkish shadow puppets that have been entertaining audiences since the Ottoman era. These characters are fundamental to Turkish shadow plays, a type of entertainment that blends humor, satire, and social commentary.

Performance & Technique: Shadow puppetry involves manipulating flat, jointed leather puppets against a backlit screen. The puppeteer, or "hayalî," voices several roles, resulting in a vibrant and fascinating performance. The plots frequently revolve around the exploits of Karagöz, a mischievous figure, and Hacivat, his more elegant and educated counterpart.

Cultural Significance: Shadow plays are a traditional aspect of Turkish folk culture, performed at festivals, religious holidays, and social gatherings. They provide information about societal standards, cultural values, and everyday living in Turkey.

Turkish Miniature Paintings

Historical Context: Miniature painting was a popular art style in the Ottoman Empire, influenced by Persian, Byzantine, and Chinese traditions. These small, detailed drawings frequently accompanied manuscripts, showing historical events, royal life, and literary works.

Techniques and Material: Miniature paintings are distinguished by their intricate detail and vivid colors. Artists employ natural paints, delicate brushes, and gold leaf to produce these exquisite paintings. The paintings frequently lack perspective, opting instead for rich representation and storytelling.

Modern Relevance: While traditional miniature painting has diminished, there is growing interest in the art form. Contemporary artists and workshops continue to investigate and recreate these techniques, incorporating them into new themes and styles.

Traditional Turkish arts and crafts showcase the country's rich cultural legacy and artistic prowess. Each art form, from the intricate patterns of carpets and pottery to the delicate strokes of calligraphy and miniatures, has a narrative to tell about creativity, tradition, and invention.

These crafts not only maintain the legacy of previous generations but also inspire and influence contemporary art and design. For anyone interested in learning about Turkish culture's depth and diversity, delving into its traditional arts and crafts is a meaningful and enriching experience. Whether you're enjoying the elegance of a silk carpet, the beauty of an Iznik tile, or the grace of a calligraphic inscription, you're tapping into a lively tradition that has stood the test of time and continues to enchant the world.

Festivals and Events to Attend

In Istanbul

Istanbul, a city that connects two continents and innumerable cultures, is a thriving hive of festivals and events all year. From music and arts to gastronomy and historical anniversaries, the city's calendar is jam-packed with events that appeal to a wide range of interests and preferences. These festivals and events not only reflect the city's rich cultural legacy, but also bring residents and visitors together to celebrate art, history, and community. Here's a complete list of the most intriguing and engaging festivals and events to visit in Istanbul.

Istanbul Music Festival

The Istanbul Music Festival is one of Turkey's most prominent classical music festivals, hosted yearly by the Istanbul Foundation for Culture and Arts (IKSV). The festival, founded in 1973, has grown to become a major cultural event, attracting world-renowned performers and orchestras.

Highlights:

Concerts & Performances: The festival offers a broad program of concerts, including symphonies, chamber music, and solo performances by foreign and Turkish players.

Performances are held at historical and modern locations in Istanbul, including the Hagia Irene Museum, Lütfi Kırdar Convention and Exhibition Centre, and Süreyya Opera House.

Workshops and Masterclasses: The festival also hosts workshops and masterclasses taught by renowned artists, allowing music students and aficionados to learn from the finest.

Best time to attend: The festival is normally held in June, providing an ideal opportunity to appreciate classical music in the picturesque backdrop of Istanbul's summer.

Istanbul Film Festival

IKSV organizes the Istanbul Film Festival, which is Turkey's oldest and largest international film festival. Since its start in 1982, the festival has been a prominent event for cinephiles, presenting a broad selection of films from all over the world.

Highlights:

Screenings: The festival shows nearly 200 films in a variety of categories, including feature films, documentaries, and shorts. It also hosts retrospectives and special screenings of vintage films.

Competitions: The festival offers numerous competitive sections, including the International Competition, the National Competition, and the Human Rights in Cinema Award.

Panels and Workshops: In addition to film screenings, the festival offers panel discussions, Q&A sessions with filmmakers, and workshops on various filmmaking topics.

Best time to attend: The Istanbul Film Festival is held yearly in April and provides an opportunity to see the latest in world cinema while also engaging with filmmakers and industry professionals.

Istanbul Jazz Festival

The Istanbul Jazz Festival, another IKSV event, has been promoting jazz music since 1994. The festival is noted for its diverse schedule, which includes jazz classics, contemporary musicians, and developing talent from Turkey and throughout the world.

Highlights:

Events: The festival's events encompass a wide spectrum of jazz styles, from conventional to avant-garde, and frequently incorporate fusion with other genres such as funk, soul, and world music.

Special Projects: The festival frequently commissions special projects and collaborations, which bring artists together for one-of-a-kind performances.

Open-air settings: Many concerts take place in spectacular open-air settings, including as the Harbiye Cemil Topuzlu Open-air Theatre and the Esma Sultan Mansion, providing an unforgettable musical experience.

Best time to attend: The Istanbul Jazz Festival takes place in July, making it an ideal summertime event for jazz enthusiasts.

Istanbul Biennial

IKSV organizes the Istanbul Biennial, which is one of the world's most major contemporary art events. Established in 1987, the biennial aims to bring cutting-edge contemporary art to Istanbul while also encouraging artistic conversation between cultures.

Highlights:

Exhibitions: The biennial showcases works by contemporary artists from throughout the world, which are presented in a variety of venues throughout Istanbul, including museums, galleries, and public places.

Themes: Each biennial edition is organized around a specific subject that addresses contemporary social, political, and cultural issues.

Programs: The event will feature artist presentations, panel discussions, workshops, and guided tours, providing a holistic art experience.

Best time to attend: The Istanbul Biennial takes place every two years in September and October, providing an opportunity to discover contemporary art in the vibrant city of Istanbul.

Istanbul Tulip Festival

The Istanbul Tulip Festival, organized by the Istanbul Metropolitan Municipality, commemorates the tulip's historical and cultural significance in Turkey. The celebration turns the city's parks and gardens into a colorful display of millions of tulips.

Highlights:

Flower Displays: The festival includes breathtaking tulip displays in several parks, including Emirgan Park, Gülhane Park, and Yildiz Park. The colorful flower beds provide a stunning backdrop for leisurely walks and photo opportunities.

Cultural Events: The festival offers a variety of cultural activities, including live music concerts, traditional dance acts, and art exhibitions.

Courses & Competitions: Visitors can attend flower arranging and gardening courses, as well as enter competitions for the finest tulip images and arrangements.

Best time to attend: The Istanbul Tulip Festival is held in April, coinciding with the blossoming season of tulips, giving it a great opportunity to experience the city's natural beauty.

International Istanbul Film Festival

The International Istanbul Film Festival, also organized by IKSV, is a prominent film festival that features films from all genres and nations. The festival encourages global cinema and allows filmmakers to showcase their work to an international audience.

Highlights:

Film Screenings: The festival shows a wide range of films, including feature films, documentaries, and shorts. It also features retrospectives, tributes, and special screenings.

Competitions and Awards: The festival offers numerous competitive sections, including the International Competition, the National Competition, and the Human Rights in Cinema Award.

Workshops and Panels: In addition to film screenings, the festival hosts workshops, panel discussions, and Q&A sessions with filmmakers to help attendees gain a better knowledge of the filmmaking process.

Best time to attend: The International Istanbul Film Festival is held yearly in April, making it an ideal opportunity for film fans to discover the latest in global cinema.

Istanbul Design Biennial

The Istanbul Design Biennial, organized by IKSV, provides a forum for investigating and debating design's position in contemporary culture, society, and politics. Founded in 2012, the biennial brings together designers, architects, and thinkers from all around the world to present innovative design practices.

Highlights:

Exhibitions: The biennial showcases many fields of design, including architecture, graphic design, industrial design, and fashion. These shows are held in a variety of locations throughout Istanbul, including museums, galleries, and public areas.

Workshops and Talks: The event will feature workshops, talks, and panel discussions with designers and experts, providing insights into the newest trends and issues in the design industry.

Interactive artworks: The biennial frequently includes interactive artworks and public interventions to engage visitors and inspire involvement.

Best time to attend: The Istanbul Design Biennial takes place every two years in October and November, offering a chance to investigate the interaction of design and current culture.

Istanbul Coffee Festival

The Istanbul Coffee Festival celebrates coffee culture by bringing together coffee connoisseurs, baristas, and roasters from all over the world. The event focuses on the art and science of coffee production, from bean to cup.

Highlights:

Coffee Tastings: The festival provides a variety of coffee tastings, allowing guests to try new brews and learn about diverse coffee-making techniques.

Workshops and Demonstrations: Coffee specialists and baristas teach and demonstrate brewing techniques, latte art, and coffee roasting.

Live Music and Performances: The festival's live music performances create a lively and joyous environment.

Best time to attend: The Istanbul Coffee Festival is held yearly in September, providing an ideal opportunity for coffee enthusiasts to indulge in their passion and explore new flavors.

Eid Celebrations.

Eid al-Fitr and Eid al-Adha are significant religious festivals observed by Muslims all over the world. In

Istanbul, these festivals are observed by communal prayers, feasts, and other cultural activities.

Highlights:

Eid Prayers: Large congregational prayers are held at mosques throughout the city, including large crowds at the Blue Mosque and Süleymaniye Mosque.

Family Gatherings and Feasts: Families celebrate with special meals that include traditional specialties like kebabs, baklava, and börek.

Public Events: The city hosts a variety of public events, such as concerts, shows, and fairs, which create a lively environment.

Best time to attend: Eid al-Fitr and Eid al-Adha are based on the Islamic lunar calendar, hence their dates change each year. Checking the Islamic calendar for the exact dates of these holidays is critical when arranging your vacation.

New Year's Eve Celebration

Istanbul's New Year's Eve celebrations are stunning, with fireworks, parties, and activities spread throughout the city. The city's blend of historic charm and modern vibrancy makes it an excellent site to celebrate the new year.

Highlights:

Fireworks: Major fireworks displays illuminate the sky over the Bosphorus, creating a spectacular background for the festivities.

celebrations & Events: Many hotels, restaurants, and nightclubs throw New Year's Eve celebrations, with entertainment ranging from live music to DJ sets.

Taksim Square and Nişantaşıare: popular gathering places for public celebrations, with street entertainers and seasonal decorations adding to the atmosphere.

Best time to attend: New Year's Eve, December 31st, is the ideal time to soak in Istanbul's festive energy and celebrate the new year in style.

Istanbul's varied assortment of festivals and events offers a vibrant and interesting cultural experience for both visitors and locals. From the classical elegance of the Istanbul Music Festival to the contemporary brilliance of the Design Biennial, and from the traditional charm of the Tulip Festival to the boisterous energy of New Year's Eve celebrations, there is always something spectacular going on in this vibrant city. Whether you enjoy music, films, or art, or simply want to immerse yourself in Istanbul's rich cultural tapestry, these festivals and events provide remarkable experiences that reflect the essence of this historic and multicultural metropolis.

Experience Turkish Baths (Hamams): A Journey of Relaxation and Culture.

The Turkish bath, or hammam, is more than just a place to cleanse the body; it is a historical and traditional institution that provides a one-of-a-kind cultural experience that has been a part of Turkish life for generations. The Turkish hamam emerged from Roman and Byzantine bathhouses throughout the Ottoman Empire, becoming an important social and cultural hub. Today, visiting a hammam is a must-do for anybody looking to learn about Turkish culture while also indulging in a timeless ritual of relaxation and regeneration.

The History and Cultural Significance of Hamams

The hamam notion dates back to the Roman era, and the Byzantines and Ottomans later embraced and altered the tradition. During the Ottoman time, hammams were built throughout the empire, serving not only as places to bathe but also as social hubs where people could relax, socialize, and do business. These bathhouses were painstakingly created to mirror the architectural grandeur of the time, with domed ceilings, marble interiors, and finely painted fountains.

Hamams were an important part of Ottoman civilization, providing a social place for both men and women. Pre-wedding ceremonies for brides, known as "gelin hamamı," were held at these locations, which were thought to offer therapeutic effects for both physical and mental well-being.

Structure and Layout of a Traditional Hamam

A classic Turkish hammam is made up of many distinct regions, each built for a specific stage of the bathing experience. Understanding the layout improves the experience by allowing guests to fully understand the ritualistic aspect of the bath.

The Camekan (entrance hall): Upon entering the hamam, guests are led to the camekan, a vast, generally octagonal room with a high ceiling and a central fountain. This space serves as the reception and changing room, allowing visitors to unwind before and after their bath. The walls are lined with private changing cubicles, and there are usually benches and tables for resting and drinking tea.

The Sıcaklık, or Hot Room: The hamam experience centers around the sıcaklık or hot room. This area is heated by a furnace (külhan) beneath the marble floor, generating a warm and humid atmosphere. The sıcaklık's centerpiece is the göbek taşı, a huge, heated marble platform where guests can lie down to sweat and relax. The göbek taşı is surrounded by individual washing stations with basins (kurna) and running water.

The Kurna (Wash Basin): At each washing station, there is a kurta with hot and cold water faucets. Visitors use copper or brass bowls to pour water over themselves before scrubbing and washing. The mix of steam and water opens pores and softens the skin, preparing it for exfoliation.

Soğukluk (Cooling Room): After spending time in the sıcaklık, guests proceed to the soğukluk, or cooling room. This area is slightly cooler, allowing the body to gradually return to normal temperatures. It usually has comfy chairs and little pools for a refreshing dip. Visitors can rest, consume beverages, and allow their bodies to adjust to the high heat of the hot room.

The Hamam Ritual: Step-by-Step.

A Turkish hamam involves a sequence of steps that cleanse, exfoliate, and rejuvenate the body. Each step is a sensory joy that adds to the overall sense of calm and well-being.

Preparation: Upon arrival, guests are greeted by attendants and directed to a private cubicle in the camekan to change into a pestemal (a traditional checkered or striped towel). Personal possessions can be safely stored in lockers or safes.

Relaxation in Sıcaklık: After changing, tourists enter the sıcaklık and begin sweating. Heat and humidity help to open pores and prepare the skin for the next steps. Guests usually spend 15-20 minutes reclining on the göbek taşı or at the washbasins, occasionally pouring water over themselves to stay comfortable.

The Scrub (Kese): After adequate sweating, a tilak (man attendant) or nation (female attendant) applies the kese, exfoliating scrub with a rough mitt. This aggressive scrubbing removes dead skin cells, leaving the skin feeling smooth and refreshed. The kese is a rigorous treatment that frequently reveals layers of dead skin that have accumulated over time.

Soap Massage (sabunlama): After the scrub, the attendant lathers the visitor with fragrant, foamy soap, usually with a soft cloth or sponge. The sabunlama comprises a light massage, which helps to relax the muscles and cleanse the skin. This stage is very relaxing, combining the benefits of massage with the cleansing characteristics of soap.

Rinsing: After the soap massage, guests rinse with warm water from the kurna. This final rinse removes any residual soap and exfoliated skin, leaving the body feeling cleansed and fresh.

Cooling down: After rinsing, guests head to the soğukluk to cool down. They can unwind on a comfy bench, sip a drink, and allow their bodies to adjust to normal temperatures. Some hamams provide herbal teas, fruit juices, or light snacks to help with the cooling down process.

Optional Treatments: Many hamams provide additional treatments, such as oil massages, facial masks, and hair care services. These supplementary treatments can be added to the standard hamam experience to provide a more comprehensive pampering session.

Choosing the Right Hamam

Istanbul is home to a variety of traditional and modern humans, each with its own distinct experience. Here are some of the most popular hammams in the city:

Çemberlitaş Hamam: Çemberlitaş Hamamı, one of Istanbul's oldest and most magnificent bathhouses, was built in 1584 by legendary Ottoman architect Mimar Sinan. Located in the historic center of the Grand Bazaar, this hamam boasts gorgeous Ottoman architecture and provides a traditional and authentic experience.

Ayasofya Hurrem Sultan Hamami: This hamam, located between the Hagia Sophia and the Blue Mosque, was commissioned by Sultan Suleiman the Magnificent's wife, Hurrem Sultan. Restored to its former magnificence, it now offers a luxury setting with separate parts for men and women.

Galatasaray Hamamı: Galatasaray Hamamı, founded in 1481, is located in the busy Beyoğlu area. It provides a true Hamam experience infused with historical charm and a pleasant ambiance.

Süleymaniye Hamami: This Hamam, designed by Mimar Sinan and located within the Süleymaniye Mosque complex, is unique in that it caters to couples and families, allowing men and women to bathe together in a historical environment.

Kılıç Ali Paşa Hamamı: Mimar Sinan built this hamam in the 16th century, and it is located in the Tophane area. It has recently been repaired and now provides a comfortable and soothing experience by combining historical ambiance with modern comforts.

Cağaloğlu Hamami: Cağaloğlu Hamamı is one of the last great hammams built during the Ottoman Empire, dating back to 1741. It is located in the center of Istanbul's historic peninsula and is well-known for its great architecture and royal feel.

Tips For First-Time Visitors

For those unfamiliar with the Turkish hamam experience, here are some pointers to ensure a comfortable and memorable visit:

Dress appropriately: Dress comfortably and bring a change of clothes for after your bath. Most humans supply a pestemal, however, you can bring your swimming suit if you prefer.

Stay hydrated: Drink plenty of water before and after your visit to stay hydrated, especially if the heat causes you to sweat profusely.

Be prepared to undress: In traditional hammams, it is usual to strip and only wear the given pestemal. If you're uncomfortable, certain humans let you wear a bikini.

Communicate your preferences: If you have any specific preferences or health concerns, please notify the attendants. They are there to make your visit comfortable and pleasurable.

Relax and enjoy: The hamam experience is intended to be peaceful and invigorating. Take your time, enjoy every stage of the process, and allow the attendants to lead you through the ceremony.

Benefits of a Turkish Bath

Aside from relaxation and cultural immersion, the Turkish bath has various other benefits. Here are some of the main advantages:

Skin Health: Exfoliation eliminates dead skin cells, clears clogged pores, and promotes healthier, more vibrant skin.

Muscle Relaxation: The heat and massage aid to relax the muscles, reduce stress, and enhance circulation.

Detoxification: Sweating helps to cleanse the body by removing pollutants and toxins.

Stress Relief: The tranquil setting and treatments offer a mental escape, lowering tension and boosting a sense of well-being.

Improved Circulation: The combination of heat and massage promotes blood circulation, which can improve general health and vigor.

A Turkish bath is a voyage into the heart of Turkish culture, providing a distinct combination of relaxation, regeneration, and historical immersion. Whether you opt for a traditional hammam with centuries-old architecture or a modern facility with excellent amenities, the Hamam experience will leave you feeling refreshed and revitalized. Embracing Turkish bath traditions and rituals not only cleanses your body but also connects you to a rich cultural legacy that has been passed down through generations. A visit to the hammam is a memorable experience that embodies Turkish hospitality and tradition.

Practical Information for Travel in Turkey

Turkey, a country with various landscapes, a rich history, and a vibrant culture, attracts millions of people each year. To make the most of your vacation, you must be well-prepared and knowledgeable about the practical aspects of travel in Turkey. This book includes useful information on language guidance, money management, staying connected, and emergency contacts to ensure a seamless and pleasurable vacation.

Language Tips and Useful Phrases.

Turkish is the official language in Turkey. While many tourists and younger generations understand English, knowing a few basic Turkish words might help you have a better travel experience and engage with locals.

Common Greetings and Polite Phrases:

Hello: Merhaba (MEHR-hah-bah)

Goodbye: Hoşçakal (HOSH-chah-kahl)

Please: Lütfen (LOOT-fehn)

Thank you: Teşekkür ederim (teh-SHEHK-koo-EHR eh-deh-REEM)

Yes: Evet (EH-veht)

No: Hayır (HAH-yuhr)

Excuse me / Sorry: Afedersiniz (ah-feh-DAIR-see-neez)

How are you?: Nasılsınız? (NAH-suhl-suh-nuhz)

I'm fine, thank you: İyiyim, teşekkür ederim (EE-yee-yeem, teh-SHEHK-koo-EHR eh-deh-REEM)

Useful Phrases for Getting Around:

Where is...?: ...nerede? (NEH-reh-deh)

How much does it cost?: Bu ne kadar? (BOO neh kah-DAHR)

Do you speak English?: İngilizce biliyor musunuz? (EEN-gee-leez-jeh BEE-lee-yor moo-soo-nooz)

Help!: Yardım edin! (YAHR-duhm eh-DEEN)

I need a doctor: Doktora ihtiyacım var (DOHK-toh-rah EEK-tee-YAH-juhm vahr)

Dining and Shopping Phrases:

I would like...: ...istiyorum (ees-TEE-yor-oom)

The bill, please: Hesap lütfen (heh-SAHHP LOOT-fehn)

Delicious!: Lezzetli! (LEZZ-et-lee)

Where is the market?: Pazar nerede? (PAH-zahr NEH-reh-deh)

Can you give me a discount?: İndirim yapar mısınız? (EEN-dee-reem yah-PAHR muh-suh-nuhz)

Learning these fundamental phrases can help you make more pleasant encounters while also demonstrating respect for the local culture.

Money: Currency, Tipping, and Budget

Currency: Turkey's official currency is the Turkish Lira (TRY), represented as ₺. Banknotes come in denominations of 5, 10, 20, 50, 100, and 200 lira, while coins come in denominations of 1, 5, 10, 25, and 50 kuruş, as well as 1 lira.

Currency Exchange: Currency can be exchanged in banks, exchange offices (Döviz), and hotels. Exchange offices, which are located in tourist areas and big cities, often give better rates. ATMs are extensively available and typically provide favorable exchange rates. To avoid card complications, advise your bank of your vacation plans.

Credit and debit cards: Credit and debit cards are commonly accepted at metropolitan hotels, restaurants, and shopping centers. However, it is advisable to take some cash, especially when visiting smaller towns or rural areas where card acceptance may be limited.

Tipping

Tipping is usual in Turkey, but the amount varies according to the service. Below are some general guidelines:

Restaurants: It is customary to tip 10-15% of the bill at mid-range to high-end restaurants. In smaller restaurants, rounding up the bill is usually sufficient.

Hotels: often tip bellboys and housekeeping personnel between 5 and 10 lira.

Taxis: Rounding up the fare to the closest lira is greatly appreciated.

Tour Guides and Drivers: For a day tour, tip the guide 20-50 lira and the driver 10-20 lira.

Budgeting:

Turkey provides a variety of experiences to suit different budgets. Here's a basic guide for daily expenses:

Budget Travellers: Expect to pay between 150 and 200 lira per day for hostel accommodations, food at modest restaurants, and public transportation.

Mid-Range Travellers: Budget 400-600 lira a day, which includes lodging in mid-range hotels, dining at mid-level restaurants, and visiting paid attractions.

Luxury Travellers: A daily budget of 1,000 lira or more will allow you to stay in luxury hotels, dine at good restaurants, and enjoy private tours or activities.

Staying Connected with SIM Cards and Internet Access

SIM Cards: Purchasing a local SIM card is a simple and inexpensive method to stay connected when traveling in Turkey. Turkcell, Vodafone, and Türk Telekom are among the leading mobile operators. SIM cards can be acquired at airports, mobile phone stores, or authorized dealers. You will need to provide your passport to register the SIM card.

Popular plans: Turkcell, Vodafone, and Türk Telekom provide a variety of prepaid plans that include data, talk time, and SMS. Plans normally cost between 100 and 200 lira, depending on the data allowance and validity term. Look for tourist packages that are specifically tailored for short-term tourists.

Internet Access:

Wi-Fi: Free Wi-Fi is frequently offered at hotels, cafes, restaurants, and public spaces in cities. Some places may require a password, which you can obtain from the personnel.

Mobile Data: Mobile data coverage in Turkey is generally decent, particularly in cities. Most prepaid SIM plans contain plenty of data, allowing you to stay connected while on the go.

Emergency Information and Contact Details

Emergency Numbers:

Police: 155.

Ambulance: 112.

Fire Department: 110.

Coast Guard: 158.

Forest fire: 177.

Useful Contacts:

Tourist Police: The Tourist Police offer help to visitors in a variety of languages. You can reach them at 155 from a local phone or +90 212 527 4503.

Foreign Consulates: It is useful to have contact information for your country's embassy or consulate in Turkey. The embassies are in Ankara, with consulates in Istanbul, Izmir, and other significant cities.

U.S. Embassy in Ankara: +90 312 455 5555.

British Consulate General in Istanbul: +90 212 334 6400.

German Consulate General in Istanbul: +90 212 334 6100.

French Consulate General in Istanbul: +90 212 334 8700.

Healthcare and Medical Services:

Hospitals: Turkey has a well-developed healthcare system that includes numerous governmental and private hospitals. Major cities such as Istanbul, Ankara, and Izmir have hospitals staffed by English speakers.

Pharmacies (Eczane): are generally available and can supply over-the-counter drugs and general healthcare advice. Many chemists can speak some English.

It is strongly advised to have comprehensive travel insurance that covers medical expenditures, accidents, and emergencies.

Transportation Contacts:

Istanbul Airport: +90 212 444 1442.

Sabiha Gökçen Airport: +90 216 585 5000.

Turkish State Railways (TCDD): +90 444 8233.

Istanbul Public Transportation: +90 212 245 0720.

Tourist Information Centres:

Tourist information centers offer maps, brochures, and information on area sites, events, and transportation. They are often found at airports, popular tourist destinations, and city centers.

Istanbul Tourist Information (Sultanahmet): +90 212 518 1800.

Istanbul Tourist Information (Taksim): +90 212 243 8530.

Ankara Tourist Information: +90 312 311 0849.

Electricity and voltage:

Voltage: 220 V.

Frequency: 50Hz.

Plug Types: Turkey employs Type C (Europlug) and Type F (Schuko) plugs. It is best to pack a universal adaptor to fit your electronic equipment.

Being well-prepared with useful information can greatly improve your trip experience in Turkey. From learning a few key Turkish phrases to knowing local currency and tipping practices, these pointers can help you navigate daily life with ease. Staying connected with a local SIM card and knowing important emergency contacts will allow you to explore Turkey comfortably and safely. By following this advice, you may immerse yourself in Turkey's colorful culture, history, and beauty while having a relaxing and enriching journey.

Conclusion

Traveling to Turkey is a voyage through millennia of history, varied cultures, and magnificent scenery. As you plan your trip, keep in mind these last-minute suggestions and methods to make the most of your time. This guide offers tips to make your experience as enriching and joyful as possible.

Last-Minute Tips.

Pack wisely: Turkey's climate varies substantially by region and season, so pack accordingly. Bring lightweight, breathable clothing, a hat, and sunscreen while visiting during the summer. Pack warm clothing and layers for winter, particularly in locations such as Cappadocia and the eastern provinces. Comfortable walking shoes are necessary for seeing historical sites and navigating metropolitan streets.

Currency and monetary management: Make sure you have a mix of cash and cards. While credit and debit cards are commonly accepted, certain small businesses and rural locations may only accept cash. It's a good idea to keep small amounts of Turkish Lira on hand for tips and little purchases. Inform your bank about your travel plans to avoid problems with card transactions.

Learn basic Turkish phrases: Although English is widely spoken in tourist regions, knowing a few basic Turkish words will help you communicate more effectively with locals. Simple pleasantries and courteous expressions like as "Hello" (Merhaba), "Thank you" (Teşekkür ederim), and "Please" (Lütfen) are valued.

Health precautions: Turkey has a well-developed healthcare system, however, it is always advisable to obtain travel insurance that covers medical expenses. Bring any prescriptions you need, as well as a basic first-aid kit. Stay hydrated, especially in the summer, and use caution when eating street food to avoid digestive difficulties.

Respect the local customs and etiquette: Understanding and following local norms will allow you to fit in and prevent cultural faux pas. Dress modestly when visiting religious buildings, take off your shoes before entering mosques, and always get permission before photographing people.

Safety and security: Turkey is typically safe for travelers, but it is critical to remain careful. Avoid isolated regions, especially at night, and keep an eye on your valuables while in crowded ones. Use licensed taxis or trustworthy ride-sharing services, and be wary of scams targeting visitors.

Connectivity: Stay connected by getting a local SIM card or ensuring that your mobile plan includes international roaming. Many cafes, restaurants, and hotels offer free Wi-Fi, although cellphone data might be useful for maps and translations.

Transportation Plan: Turkey's public transport network is vast and efficient. Learn about the metro, tram, and bus lines in major cities such as Istanbul and Ankara. Domestic flights are a cheap and time-saving option for longer distances.

Cultural Sensitivity: Turkey is a combination of modernism and heritage. Show respect for local customs, particularly in rural areas. Be aware of religious traditions, such as prayer times, and dress appropriately in conservative areas.

Emergency Contacts: Keep a list of emergency contact information, including your country's local embassy or consulate, as well as emergency service numbers. It's also a good idea to have the contact information for your hotel or accommodation.

How to make the most of your visit

Explore Beyond Major Cities: While Istanbul, Ankara, and Izmir are must-see destinations, don't overlook the opportunity to see Turkey's various provinces. Explore the magical landscapes of Cappadocia, the ancient remains of Ephesus, the hot baths of Pamukkale, and the pristine beaches of the Turquoise Coast.

Immerse yourself with local culture: Participating in traditional activities allows you to connect with the local culture. Attend a Whirling Dervish ritual, learn how to make Turkish coffee, or take a Turkish cookery class. These experiences provide a deeper understanding of Turkish culture and daily life.

Enjoy Turkish cuisine: Turkish cuisine is a highlight of any trip. Enjoy a variety of meals, including kebabs, mezes, baklava, and Turkish delight. Street food favorites include simit (sesame-covered bread rings) and börek (savory pastries). Visit a local market to savor fresh fruit, cheeses, and olives.

Experience the Hamam: A visit to a traditional Turkish bath, or hammam, is an unforgettable and refreshing experience. Steam, cleansing, and massage are traditional Turkish bathhouse rituals.

Attend festivals and events: Check the local calendar for festivals and activities happening during your visit. Participating in events such as the Istanbul Music Festival, the International Istanbul Film

Festival, or the vivid Tulip Festival provides a lively and immersive cultural experience.

Visit historic sites: Turkey has an abundance of historical sites. Explore the Hagia Sophia and Topkapi Palace in Istanbul, the ancient city of Troy, Göreme's rock-hewn cathedrals, and the spectacular Mount Nemrut. Each location conveys a tale about Turkey's rich and diverse history.

Take scenic drives: Renting a car allows you to explore Turkey's breathtaking scenery at your own speed. Drive along the Aegean and Mediterranean shores, over the Black Sea mountains, or across Central Anatolia's huge plains. Scenic paths provide stunning views and the chance to find hidden gems.

Engage with locals: Turkish people are renowned for their hospitality. Take the time to interact with the people, whether through a talk in a café, shopping at local markets, or staying in family-run guesthouses. These exchanges can provide useful information and make your trip more memorable.

Embrace the pace of Turkish life: Take a minute to relax and enjoy the slower pace of Turkish life. Enjoy a cup of Turkish tea or coffee, unwind in a park, or observe the world from a classic teahouse. Embracing the local rhythm can improve your trip experience.

Capture the Moment: Turkey provides several photo options, ranging from crowded bazaars and ancient ruins to breathtaking vistas and vivid street scenes. Take plenty of images to record the essence of your journey, but also allow yourself to fully engage in the experience without the lens.

Traveling to Turkey is a journey full of historical wonders, cultural encounters, and magnificent natural scenery. Following these last-minute recommendations and making the most of your stay will ensure a memorable and enlightening experience. Whether you're exploring Istanbul's bustling streets, admiring ancient ruins, or savoring the flavors of Turkish food, each moment in Turkey provides a unique view into a country that connects continents and cultures. Embrace variety, interact with locals, and immerse yourself in this intriguing land's rich heritage. Your Turkish trip awaits, delivering wonderful memories and a greater appreciation for one of the world's most alluring countries.

Appendix

Useful Apps for Traveling in Turkey

Google Maps

Description: Essential for navigation, finding attractions, and planning routes.

Features: Offline maps, real-time traffic updates, directions for driving, walking, and public transit.

Moovit

Description: Public transportation guide.

Features: Real-time updates, transit schedules, route planning for buses, trams, and metro.

XE Currency

Description: Currency converter.

Features: Real-time exchange rates, offline mode, multiple currency conversion.

BiTaksi

Description: Taxi booking app in Turkey.

Features: GPS tracking, fare estimation, cash/card payment options.

Getir

Description: On-demand delivery service for groceries and essentials.

Features: Fast delivery, wide product range, user-friendly interface.

Turkish Airlines

Description: Official app of Turkish Airlines.

Features: Flight booking, check-in, flight status, and notifications.

Istanbul Kart

Description: Istanbul's public transportation card app.

Features: Balance inquiry, top-up options, trip history.

TripAdvisor

Description: Travel planning and review app.

Features: Reviews, travel guides, hotel and restaurant bookings.

Frequently Asked Questions (FAQs)

What is the best time to visit Turkey?

- Answer: The best time to visit Turkey is during the spring (April to June) and autumn (September to November) when the weather is mild and pleasant, making it ideal for sightseeing and outdoor activities.

Is Turkey safe for tourists?

- Answer: Yes, Turkey is generally safe for tourists. However, it's important to stay aware of your surroundings, avoid political demonstrations, and follow local news for any travel advisories.

Do I need a visa to visit Turkey?

- Answer: Many nationalities require a visa to enter Turkey. Visitors can apply for an e-Visa online before arrival. Check the Turkish government's e-Visa website for eligibility and application details.

What are the must-visit attractions in Istanbul?

- Answer: Must-visit attractions in Istanbul include the Hagia Sophia, Topkapi Palace, Blue Mosque, Grand Bazaar, Bosphorus Strait, and the Basilica Cistern. Each offers a unique glimpse into the city's rich history and culture.

How can I stay connected in Turkey?

- Answer: Purchasing a local SIM card from major providers like Turkcell, Vodafone, or Türk Telekom is recommended for staying connected. Alternatively, many cafes, hotels, and public spaces offer free Wi-Fi.

Travel Checklist

Documents and Essentials:

- Passport and copies
- Visa (if required)
- Travel insurance
- Flight tickets
- Accommodation confirmations
- Itinerary and reservation details
- Emergency contacts

Electronics:

- Smartphone and charger
- Portable power bank
- Camera and accessories
- Universal travel adapter
- Headphones

Clothing:

- Weather-appropriate clothing
- Comfortable walking shoes
- Swimwear

- Light jacket or sweater
- Hat and sunglasses

Toiletries:

- Toothbrush and toothpaste
- Shampoo and conditioner
- Soap or body wash
- Deodorant
- Sunscreen
- Personal medications

Miscellaneous:

- Travel guidebook
- Reusable water bottle
- Snacks
- Travel pillow and eye mask
- Small daypack or backpack

Travel Itinerary

3-Day Travel Itinerary

Day 1: Istanbul Highlights

Morning: Visit Hagia Sophia and Blue Mosque.

Afternoon: Explore Topkapi Palace and its gardens.

Evening: Stroll through the Grand Bazaar and have dinner in Sultanahmet.

Day 2: Bosphorus and Modern Istanbul

Morning: Take a Bosphorus cruise.

Afternoon: Visit Dolmabahçe Palace and the Istanbul Modern Art Museum.

Evening: Dinner in Taksim Square and explore Istiklal Street.

Day 3: Historical and Cultural Experience

Morning: Visit the Basilica Cistern.

Afternoon: Explore the Spice Bazaar and Rustem Pasha Mosque.

Evening: Enjoy a traditional Turkish bath at Ayasofya Hurrem Sultan Hamami.

5-Day Travel Itinerary

Day 1-3: Follow the 3-Day Itinerary Above

Day 4: Day Trip to Cappadocia

Early Morning: Fly to Nevşehir or Kayseri.

Morning: Explore the Göreme Open-Air Museum.

Afternoon: Visit the underground city of Derinkuyu or Kaymakli.

Evening: Return flight to Istanbul.

Day 5: Istanbul's Asian Side

Morning: Ferry to Kadıköy and explore the local markets.

Afternoon: Visit the Çamlıca Hill for panoramic views.

Evening: Dinner in Moda and return to the European side by ferry.

7-Day Travel Itinerary

Day 1-5: Follow the 5-Day Itinerary Above

Day 6: Ephesus and Pamukkale

Early Morning: Fly to Izmir.

Morning: Explore the ancient city of Ephesus.

Afternoon: Visit the House of Virgin Mary and drive to Pamukkale.

Evening: Relax in the thermal pools of Pamukkale.

Day 7: Return to Istanbul and Final Exploration

Morning: Fly back to Istanbul.

Afternoon: Visit the Chora Church and its stunning mosaics.

Evening: Enjoy a farewell dinner on a rooftop terrace with views of the Bosphorus.

Made in the USA
Monee, IL
08 November 2024

69629392R00109